# Facing Our Cumulative Developmental Trauma

*An Interpersonal/Relational Approach*

**Lawrence E. Hedges,** PhD., PsyD., ABPP

This book is dedicated to the clients and therapists who over a forty-year period have come to my consulting room to teach me about Cumulative Developmental Trauma and the ways we have of overcoming it.

# Table of Contents

## An Interpersonal/Relational Approach to Trauma

The Force is With Us! • Life's Traumatic Experiences • Some Historical Notes • Hold It! Let's Go Back a Few Steps • Personal Identity as Traumatically Constructed • The Post-Modern, Social Construction Perspctive • Let's Start at the Beginning • Listening Relationally to Trauma • Resistance to Re-Experiencing Trauma • Reality: The Therapist's Dilemma • De-Centering from Our Own Subjectivity: Barbara Kingslover • Some Imprecise Definitions • Some Ordinary People

## Developmental Fears and Cumulative Trauma

Cumulative Developmental Trauma • Listening to Cascading Traumatic Experiences: September 11, 2001 • Overcoming Our Relational Fears: An Overview • Considering Seven Universal Developmental Fears • The Body-Mind-Relationship (BMR) Connection

## Re-Experiencing Cumulative Trauma in Relational Psychotherapy: Brief Illustrations

"I was trained to be a monster" • "I want you dead so I can be myself" • "With everyone I am compelled to 'service Mother'" • "I had to die for Mother" • "I saw Barbara with straw hat and feather boa" • "The doctor is interfering with my birth" • So Much to Do, So Little Time • Dream: "The Invasion of the Chili Pepper Monster"

# Foreword

Creative thinkers come along rarely. When they do, in whatever their field, they show us new ways of relating to our lives. They take the familiar and make it unfamiliar; then they show us how to integrate their insights so that the unfamiliar can become a new familiar.

This is not a process that is universally appreciated. Frequently, the creative thinker is perceived as primarily saying "you are wrong," something almost no one likes to hear. Regardless of the subject, regardless of the century, he or she is almost always told to be quiet and to go away.

Dr. Larry Hedges will not be quiet and has not gone away. For decades, Larry has sought the answer to one of life's key questions: How can we help others through their deep personal struggles without scaring them off by the way we offer them the tools they need to move forward? This question is central to love, to intimacy, and to psychotherapy.

*Facing Our Cumulative Developmental Traumas* provides meaningful, creative, and useful and usable answers to that question.

The book notes that the vulnerable nature of being human ensures that everyone will endure trauma, and that everyone will develop psychological scars as they grapple with this trauma. Handled well, those scars develop into emotional strengths, including the ability to love deeply. Unfortunately, not all scars are handled well—either by ourselves or by others.

As in every age, we live in a time of great personal pain—which

Larry puts into a new light. For starters, he says that "trauma and post-traumatic experience are not only universal, but necessary for normal and healthy growth." This perspective is tremendously empowering, as it helps people see that painful experiences do not define them, but rather are part of who they are. Thus we see that people are bigger than their experiences of exploitation, neglect, or sadism. People are bigger than their trauma.

Following and updating Freud, Larry reminds us that when we discuss trauma, subjective meanings are far more important than facts. Again, this is empowering for those who suffer, because it puts them in the center of the experience. "This happened" is replaced by "this happened to me." The question that logically follows from the latter approach is "what was and is your experience of what happened?" Or to put it another way, "what meanings, predictions, and unique interpretations did you create in response to your experience?" Each of us lives with the answers to that question.

This is a tremendous contrast to the identity politics that plague America (and psychotherapy) today. That contemporary approach encourages people to see themselves as members of aggrieved groups who need to battle each other for social and material resources (respect, funding, government listing as a minority needing affirmative action, etc.). In this telling, the most important thing we can know about someone is the group to which they belong, and the struggles they have had as a member of that group.

Political correctness is a predictable aspect of this orientation, as victimhood is valorized and personal truth is replaced by stereotype. The ever-growing popularity of the addiction model among both therapists and the public is another aspect of this. Virtually any compelling, self-damaging attachment is now labelled an addiction by many people. The one-size-fits-all 12-step approach is now used to address undesirable relationships with shopping, pornography, and almost everything else.

As I supervise therapy cases around the country, I see a trend in which therapists want to know what category their patient belongs to, just as I see therapists encouraging spouses to see each other as members of categories. Patients or spouses are "women," or "gay," or "Italian-American," or "adult children of alcoholics." Somehow each of these enormous categories is supposed to be homogeneous in meaningful ways. And so therapists are actually talking to patients about the *kind of person* the patient or their spouse are.

Therapy needs to be doing exactly the opposite—discouraging people from seeing themselves or each other as members of categories, and encouraging people to see themselves or each other as unique individuals. Larry's ideas about intersubjectivity and relational psychotherapy are a welcome and very practical reminder of why this is important. This book, along with most of his others, offers specific steps people can take to implement this more humane, intersubjective and relational perspective.

But Larry is no naïve Flower Child, no conflict-avoidant Good Boy. He is a loving, generous man who is tough as nails.

One must be tough to live with enormous volumes of human suffering—especially the way that he does it. "Bring it on" (said gently, not brazenly) might be his motto. This is all the more impressive when you realize that his idea of therapy is to help people re-experience their pain, and for him to do so along with the patient. Not to *imagine* it, nor to *intellectualize* it via convenient categories (as in "I know when people are raped they generally feel X"), but to *feel* the patient's uniquely constructed pain as she or he feels it while reconstituting it.

Indeed, Larry has a radical concept of relationships, in their context for both trauma and for healing. He brilliantly observes that both our low-grade daily tensions and our childhood fear reflexes develop within the confines of intimate relationships. Therefore it is only within relationships that we can resolve our habits of daily tension and fear reflexes. In this book, Larry shows how.

For Larry, the body is a key part of any discussion of trauma and our recovery from it. Our capacity for sensation lives in our bodies, of course, as do the sequelae of our traumatic experiences. Again, Larry's focus on understanding how each person interprets—and therefore creates—the events experienced by that person's body, whether conscious or unconscious, is both respectful and deeply reasonable, a perfect foundation for deeply effective therapy or intimate relating.

Sexuality, of course, is a lived reality of our bodies. "Great sex" is an experience many of us crave—made almost impossible by our response to the "normal" traumas of childhood, adolescence, and adulthood. We sacrifice "great sex" as part of our accommodation to painful pasts—deciding that we are, variously, too clumsy, not attractive, not sufficiently womanly, the wrong gender or ethnicity, etc. Mostly, we sacrifice our sexuality to the idea that we will lose another's approving gaze if we expose ourselves too honestly.

Too much of contemporary discourse about enhancing sexual enjoyment is about improving genital "function" or acquiring new sex toys or positions. In reality, therapy for sexual difficulties should focus primarily on supporting people's self-acceptance and helping them locate and resolve internal challenges to that self-acceptance. Larry's ideas in this book offer just such support.

Readers will also be enlightened as Larry discusses what he calls our Seven Deadly Fears. I think of these as everyone's existential challenges, inevitable problems each of us must resolve in order to continue our adult development and enjoy life. Larry finds a unique fine line between endless anguish over existential facts (for example, that we can't completely protect our loved ones from pain), and the depression that comes from passively accepting these truths without doing the necessary psychological work to creatively integrate them.

In this book as in all his work, Larry urges us to be fully human, cheering us on while simultaneously mourning our early trauma with us. You will enjoy his deeply optimistic and loving vision while you read this book. You have chosen the guide for your next psychological and emotional adventure wisely.

–Marty Klein, Ph.D
Palo Alto, CA May 18, 2015

# Author's Preface

It has now become clear that Cumulative Developmental Trauma is universal. That is, there is no way to grow up and walk the planet without being repeatedly swallowed up by emotional and relational demands from other people. When we become confused, frightened, and overwhelmed our conscious and unconscious minds seek remedies to deal with the situation. Unfortunately many of the solutions developed in response to intrusive events turn into habitual fear reflexes that get in our way later in life, giving rise to post-traumatic stress and relational inhibitions. This book is about identifying the kinds of frightening relational situations faced by all of us in the course of growing up and then working toward resolving the post-traumatic stresses that remain to haunt our bodies, minds, and relationships. Therefore, I have written this book with something of interest to everybody.

Readers who are psychotherapists and have a special interest in understanding and working with traumatic and post-traumatic stress may be interested in the four appendices clarifying the epistemological and technical backdrop of Interpersonal/Relational Psychotherapy.

I hope you find this book enjoyable and useful.

Larry Hedges
Orange, California

# Part One

# An Interpersonal/Relational Approach to Trauma

## The Force is With Us!

Something within us wants to be set free. Set free from what?

From the inner bonds and shackles that hold us captive to ourselves.

Myths from around the world have portrayed this journey—the journey of "the hero with 1000 faces."

Whether we must slay dangerous dragons, risk our life capturing the golden fleece, pass through treacherous narrows, resist the temptations of the terrifying sirens, or plunge headlong into the vast unknown universe, we somehow know that "the force" is with us in our journey.

The heroine finds herself surrounded by hordes of monsters and evil-doers, trudging through the steamy pits of Hell, and cursed by the envious gods. But the perilous Heroine's Journey—a saga not for the feint-hearted—continues in face of life's ongoing challenges and traumas.

This book is about freeing ourselves from the cumulative effects of our life's many relational traumas and the after-effects of those traumas that continue to constrict our capacities for creative, spontaneous, and passionate living.

Our traumatic wounds were caused by breakdowns in human

relationships. Our healing depends upon achieving safe and reliable relationships in which we can re-experience those wounding moments and set ourselves free from their constrictions.

# Life's Traumatic Experiences

We have all endured a lifetime of traumas, even though we may have ignored or attempted to deny or pass over their emotional impact on us. When most of us consider the kinds of traumas we have experienced and compare them with what victims of genocide, war, plagues, tsunamis, life-threatening diseases, disabling accidents, insurmountable poverty, racial prejudice, or severe childhood abuse have endured we count ourselves fortunate.

Yet we know that we, too, have suffered greatly in the course of growing up and establishing a good life for ourselves. While we have no desire to cast ourselves into the role of victims, neither does it help to pretend that we have not had our share of traumatic suffering—the impact of which lingers on to haunt our everyday lives and relationships in many ways.

Psychological and neuropsychological research over the past few decades into severe trauma and post-traumatic experience has fortunately given us many new insights into the nature of trauma and made clear that trauma and post-traumatic experience is not only universal but *necessary* for normal and healthy growth!

Historically, this is the way psychological studies have proceeded. Some extreme or "pathological condition" comes to the attention of clinicians and researchers. Then careful study of how the "pathological condition" operates shows us a new aspect of human life that is universal, but that had not yet been so visible in ordinary everyday experience.

An entirely new paradigm is now emerging for our understanding of the universality and the normality of traumatic and post-traumatic experience. Thus the formerly pathological Post-Traumatic Stress Disorder (PTSD) is now being referred to simply as Post-Traumatic Experience (PTE). We now understand there is a continuum of traumatic and post-traumatic experience — from ordinary and developmentally normal and expectable traumas and cumulative strain traumas to highly impactful extreme forms of focal and intrusive traumas.

Traumatic experiences can enhance our development by providing seemingly insurmountable challenges or they can devastate us at any stage of life. But the relational traumas that occur in early life are particularly devious in that they lay a faulty foundation for later growth experiences. *But—whether earlier or later, whether mild, moderate, severe, focal or cumulative—the essential nature of trauma in human life remains the same, and the universal after-effects are by now well-known and predictable.*

## Some Historical Notes

Sigmund Freud's seminal discovery was that, given a favorable relational situation, a person could gain access — through inter-personal mirroring processes — to the ways that her internal world of experience had become structured and to the ways that she could free herself from her developmentally structured bondage.

More than a century has passed with many brilliant people following Freud in attempting to define the nature of the human mind and how we as individuals can learn to transcend the effects of our necessarily limiting developmental relational experiences. Over the years many theories, traditions, and techniques have evolved.

Throughout all of this theoretical and clinical development it has always been understood that early traumatic experiences have a profound effect on later life experiences. But the exact ways that traumatic experience *contributes* to human growth as well as gives rise to crippling constrictions and inhibitions has continued to elude us. That is, it has continued to elude us until recent technological advances have made possible a vast expansion of knowledge.

In the last three decades we have come to learn more about human genetics, infant experience, brain and mental development and the central role of interpersonal relational experience in human mental development than we have known since the beginning of time. This new knowledge has massive implications for the universal nature of trauma. For example, it is now clear to us that *each individual human brain is actually structured according to early emotional-relational experiences that are and are not available in infancy*. And that this early interpersonal structuring of the brain and the entire neurological system provides the essential foundation for all later mental development. That is, each human brain and neurological system is absolutely unique. And each person—based on early interpersonal emotional regulation and mirroring processes—develops her own internal, subjective world of experience that will guide her in her future development.

What has slowly emerged in our exponentially expanding awareness of human mental development, is the central role of trauma in structuring each person's internal world of subjective experience. As I will show shortly, the foundational aspects of *all* mental development are essentially molded by traumatic experience!

In common language, a traumatic experience is something terrible that happens to you—a horrible, overwhelming *and psychological event* that leaves you traumatized. However, in medical terms inherited from Ancient Greece trauma does not refer to the blow itself or to the invasive event per se, but rather to *the body's healing response to the blow*—that is "trauma" refers to the processes involved in healing the wound. The American Psychological Association still defines psychological trauma as "an emotional response to a terrible event like an accident, rape or natural disaster" (online definition). It follows then, that in our efforts to recover from various traumas we are not trying to make the original blow or event diminish or disappear because we can't—rather we are trying to overcome the cumulative effects of our internally structured responses to interpersonal blows that remain in our inner subjective worlds constricting our personal paths into the future.

## Hold It! Let's Go Back a Few Steps

The great debate among psychologists and philosophers of the nineteenth century had to do with which was more important in the development of human beings—the influences of nature or the influences of nurture? Sigmund Freud felt that his greatest contribution to human thought was the awareness that from earliest development a third influence, infinitely more powerful than either nature or nurture—though limited by both—was the gradual emergence of what he called the "internal world." That is, the raw ingredients of the "human mind"—taken from nature and nurture— become rapidly organized by each infant into patterns of expectation and responsiveness that exert powerful influences on subsequent mental development.

Freud understood that it was the social nature of our species, and the gift of being able to pass socially-derived learning down the generations through the cultivation of emotionally-derived symbols and culture, that constituted the genius of our species. The socialization processes necessary for the mind of a child to enter the complexities of human culture necessarily required learning, relearning, and reformatting and then learning again. This relentlessly required relearning and reformatting process is demanded by internal and external intrusions into the way the child and later the adult has structured her inner subjective world of experience at that point in time. A creative response on her part—using whatever resources she might have available at the moment—aims at overcoming the effects of that intrusion either by smoothly *assimilating* the new information, or by traumatically *accommodating* the demands of the intrusion by re-arranging the established patterns of her internal world. Thus, *assimilation of* and *accommodation to novel learning situations are understood to be universal and normal developmental processes. Assimilation does not require a traumatic repair or reconstruction process but accommodation does.* The people who found their way to Freud's consulting room brought various patterns of traumatically generated accommodations for his consideration.

Freud aimed his curiosity not so much toward the internal or external cause of the intrusion—the traumatic event itself—but toward *the way the person's unconscious mind responded to or internally re-organized a pattern of reparative, re-orienting responses. The relational patterns thus built might be developmentally enhancing or seriously inhibiting.* Freud was the first to realize that from a therapeutic standpoint the intrusive event itself was not so important as the way the person experienced and internally organized the effects of that event.[1] Freud's *focus as a therapist in creating a healing relational atmosphere* needed to be not on the blow or the symptoms per se, but rather *on the traumatic response—that is, on unraveling the complex web of personal internalized meanings generated by the intrusion.* Contemporary Interpersonal/Relational Psychotherapy continues in this essentially Freudian tradition of privileging personal meanings over the facts of the traumatic event— the most important *therapeutic* insight of Freud's life.

The point here is that in normal developmental learning a child is constantly required to assimilate new information into her already existing internal world and to accommodate—to reorganize established features of it—in order to satisfy intrusive internal or external demands. *This process of internally re-organizing one's patterns of relational experience in order to accommodate the intrusive demands of reality is essentially the process of healing referred to in medicine and psychology as trauma.* However, like all healing processes a scar remains to tell the story. The psychological scar is a pattern of habitual interpersonal emotional responses developed to accommodate impingement in an earlier interpersonal situation. But, unfortunately, previously established emotional relatedness patterns often do not serve well in later interpersonal situations. This was Freud's essential definition of "neurosis".

As a practicing physician, Freud early on focused his *treatment approach to crippling neurotic patterns* in the person' ongoing internal life as opposed to whatever its sources might have been in traumatically intrusive events. Only a century later have we been able to see the human imperative of the interpersonal or intersubjective field—that is, that the life of a human subject is at all times immersed in a field of social (interpersonal) or intersubjective relations. And therefore, that *all* intrusions into individual psychic life requiring accommodation, whether extreme or more developmentally ordinary, impact the development of the individual human body and mind and must, therefore, be understood as traumatic and taken into account in therapy.

# Personal Identity as Traumatically Constructed

Almost as a sidebar, it is important to note that personal identifications—gender and otherwise—exist as internal defensive structures that are also traumatically constructed. As Anna Freud first pointed out in her classic study of "identification with the aggressor" (1937), even the most favorable intrusions provided by careful and loving parental guidance and ministration are often experienced by the developing child as traumatic intrusions into his or her internal spontaneously arriving motivations. She saw these internal identifications as derived from a traumatically-generated interpersonal defensive process. Alice Balint (1943) further developed the understanding that human identifications are based upon internalizing the effects of experienced interpersonal intrusions into personally organized subjective worlds of experience.

Likewise, those who study gender identifications indicate that binary cultural gender definitions traumatically intrude into the young child's omnipotent and omniscient sense of self, i.e., "I can be anything and everything not merely a boy or a girl." Following Freud, Anna Freud, and Alice Balint we can see that the individual human mind is structured according to its own constitution as determined by nature and nurture as well as according to its own internal relational patterns and identify structures as established by fateful encounters with influential interpersonally generated forces stronger than itself.

## The Post-Modern, Social Construction Perspective

We now recognize that the most complex phenomenon in the known universe is the human mind—and that the human mind is infinitely complex. As beings on this planet we have evolved over millions of years in what physicists tell us are ten or more dimensions—though we can only consciously perceive four of them. The implications of this new knowledge are staggering in the realization that many of the processes that have gone into our human and pre-human evolution and that guide our individual development and are critically influential in later dynamic processes of change will inevitably and forever remain unknown and unknowable. This understanding calls for a new approach to knowledge.

I recall once having heard the quantum physicist Heinz Pagels remark, "In trying to picture the strangeness of the quantum universe that we live in the question is, are we like Piaget's children of various ages who were presented with a number of bottles of different sizes and shapes on the shelf all filled to the same level with water. When the children were asked, 'do the bottles contain the same or different amounts of water?', the older more experienced children were able to give more accurate answers than the younger ones. Or are we like our domestic pets who live in a world not of their own construction or understanding—but despite that fact have learned very well how to live comfortably within it and to work it to their advantage? We do not have the answer to this question (personal communication)."

Therefore, in considering the infinite complexities of human existence, rather than attempting to theorize in the "modernist" tradition of seeking to determine "the truths of the human mind," we can now recognize that we are living in a "post-modern" era which recognizes our human world to be essentially socially constructed by somewhat arbitrary conventions we call language and culture. At this point in time effective research and practice necessarily follows an epistemology informed by evolution, relativity, quantum leaps, nonlinear systems, and socially constructed cultural and linguistic systems, as well as *somewhat arbitrary human vantage points or perspectives from which to observe, in whatever ways we can, ourselves and the subjectively constructed worlds we live in.* Whatever else is active in determining our collective and individual existences remains unknown and, in principle, forever unknowable and has been labeled by Wilfred Bion as "O" (1992). But there are other ways to conceptualize the infinite unknown of human experience.

William James in his *Varieties of Religious Experience, a Study in Human Nature* (1901-02) has given us a way to think about human nature in relation to the "mysterious beyond." Starting with the same supposition that Bion did some years later, James believes that what is originally given to the human species as real is the biologically-based capacity for sensations. Subsequently human linguistic and cultural history as well as childrearing practices have structured how a member of the species is to come to experience important survival realities.

We now know from DNA decoding that human nature over millions of years and even after the exodus from northeast Africa some 50,000 years ago has continued to evolve vigorously and robustly (Wade 2006, 2014). While some of that evolution may simply be genes switching "on" and "off" so that adaptation to environmental features can be made, other natural selection features have involved cultural institutions that appear in turn to have called for genetic modifications. Further, it is now clear from physics that we have evolved in ten or more dimensions though we can only perceive four of those—height, width, depth, and time (Greene, 2003, 2004).

Prior to these contemporary findings, James intuited that there was a vast unknown beyond what human perception was regularly capable of discerning. Yet knowledge of these other dimensions of human existence has been occasionally grasped by different individuals and by different social groups over the course of human history. This point has been repeatedly emphasized by J. Chilton Pearce in his *Crack in the Cosmic Egg* and subsequent treatises on evolutionary forces (1970, revised 2002).

James' eighteen lectures delivered at the University of Scotland in Edinburg in 1901 and 1902 form a detailed and scholarly account surveying different types of religious experience reported by individuals and cultural groups throughout time. His conclusion is that since time immemorial humans have known that they emanate from other realms than those that can be perceived by the culturally created four survival dimensions. Humans know this because of their capacity for biologically-based sensations that are founded in other dimensions, other realms of unperceived realities. While James acknowledges his own cultural proclivities for formulation of religious ideas and images based in Western Civilization Christianity, he makes clear that each cultural/religious group throughout the world has done its best to formulate the known but mysterious dimensions beyond in categories, dogmas and institutions that reflect the conditions of their environmental/cultural evolutionary heritage. That is, revelations of the beyond necessarily take on images and narrations compatible with the four-dimensional cultural formulations that have preceded them in each cohesive socio-cultural group.

The visual metaphor that James employs suggests that we live in a culturally bound set of four-dimensional perceptions but that our biological knowledge through sensations goes considerably beyond these barriers. Our sensorial knowledge of our more complex beingness presses us ever toward knowledge of dimensions on the other side of our cultural/perceptual barrier. In his metaphor he speaks of the mysterious beyond as "thither." And our cultural four-dimensional knowledge as the "hither". He speaks of an opening or door through which from time to time humans—individuals and groups—manage some direct experience of and identification with the mysterious beyond. But when individuals or groups attempt to describe the thither in the hither they are bound to the four dimensional cultural linguistic systems that have formed their conscious minds. Therefore, people from different religious/cultural groups necessarily describe their revelations in very different terms. James details the ways in which this knowledge has become institutionalized in various cultures through practices and dogmas as well as the ways in which individuals and groups continue to press against the established dogmas into experiences of alternate states of consciousness and how those alternate states become imaged and communicated. James believes that religious experience is not an anachronistic cultural practice doomed to wither away over time, but rather that resonates with our deepest sensations and will continue to do so. Like Bion, James became very interested in the ways that mystics have attempted to describe their experiences of the mysterious beyond.

Science writer Nicholas Wade in three remarkable books (2006, 2009. 2014) has collected scientific evidence from many disciplines that has much to say about where we are now in the course of human evolution. Like Bion and James he too cites religious experience as a vital aspect of human evolution—one that is aimed at understanding the vast mysterious unknown. Wade's views highlight the importance of cultural institutions that have arisen in various parts of the world in response to human adaptational needs. Wade's knowledge of DNA allows him to formulate that the gene pool among all humans is essentially the same. However, due to adaptations in institutional life in different locales certain variations have had local survival value and the forces of natural selection have continued to operate—even in the last 50,000 years. His thesis is that while all humans have essentially the same genes for social behavior, the differential survival value of various cultural institutions has led to different relational habits and forms of consciousness in the five continental groups as well as other smaller groups.

Another contribution to our evolving sense of invisible realities that affect human experience is psychoanalyst Elizabeth

Lloyd Mayer's recent book, *Extraordinary Knowing: Science, Skepticism and the Inexplicable Powers of the Human Mind*, that reports on a large and significant research project conducted by a group of psychoanalysts into experiences of knowing that defy our current ways of understanding the universe—that go beyond the four survival dimensions created by human language and culture. This remarkable study may well point the way into future understanding of human relationships—including the therapeutic relationship.

The bottom line of the post-modern social construction perspective is that we live in a world that's much vaster than we now know or are ever likely to know about. The importance of the post-modern social construction approach to understanding cumulative developmental trauma will become clear later as we discuss generating useful perspectives from which to listen to people who come to our consulting rooms.

## Let's Start at the Beginning

We are living a promise which is as mysterious and old as life itself. The promise is that if we reach out into our environment with interest, curiosity, and enthusiasm our reaching will be seen, recognized, and appropriately engaged to produce a sense of safety and personal growth. In each of our lives this promise has been fulfilled many times, but our reaching out for enlivening connections has often been painfully thwarted.

Since the earliest replications of DNA molecules, the forces of life have been adequately met with enough environmental engagement to produce the pageant of the species. At the human level this life promise extends from the moment of conception. A womb is waiting to receive the zygote. At birth, mother's arms, eyes, breasts, and caresses greet the child. Behind the mother stands the nurturing couple, the human family, and a society that aims at making life safe and rewarding for each human being. But we know, despite these provisions and this promise, serious obstacles and frustrations arise at every turn. Fortunately, evolution has prepared us to deal with many kinds of relational obstacles—but, as we shall see, each solution comes with a price. And with growth and development the price becomes cumulative.

Both processes of assimilation and accommodation are assumed to be normal and universal—that is, both can provide healthy and strengthening challenges. But accommodations can also serve as traumatic impingements in relational development that become devastatingly cumulative. *The subject of this book is setting up a relational scene for identifying and overcoming these cumulative relational traumas.*

There are, of course, degrees of intrusive traumatic impingement and there are many degrees of individual preparedness for impingement that can either stimulate challenges to creative growth or precipitate disastrous and defeating collapses. And, of course, the impact of various kinds of overstimulating intrusions are different at different times and at different stages of human development. Furthermore, different people respond differently to the same impinging forces—one may have an assimilating response while another may have a traumatically accommodating experience. These many possibilities will be illustrated later. But for now it is sufficient to have some concept of how we can grow from assimilating relational obstacles as well as how we come to develop internalized challenges and/or cumulative crushing and shaming collapses as a result of accommodating overwhelming negative relational experiences.[2]

## Listening Relationally to Trauma

Interpersonal/Relational Psychotherapy is about two people attempting to take personal responsibility for the lingering *internal* effects of their past traumas—whether they be developmental, cumulative strain, or focal trauma. In contrast, the work of the trauma community tends to place emphasis on defining the realistic and narrational features of traumatic moments and their after-effects and then to promote actions to overcome, master, or heal the post-traumatic effects or symptoms.[3]

Interpersonal/Relational Psychotherapy moves, as far as is possible, in the direction of encouraging the gradual psychological and physiological *re-experiencing* of earlier traumas in the context of a safe, emotionally intimate, and supportive here-and-now therapeutic relationship. Psychological and physical re-experiencing of traumatic moments—as much as is possible and within a time frame that is bearable—is generally encouraged based upon the assumption that the terror and helplessness—including rage, shame, guilt, denial, and dissociation—of prior traumatic moments can be meaningfully integrated or managed better within the context of a later, emotionally intimate, safe, and supportive relational environment. This occurs with the traumatized person presumably having a more mature mind than she/he did at the time of the original traumatic moment so as to be able to understand what is going on more or less as it is being re-lived in the ongoing intersubjective therapeutic context.[4]

The trauma community is generally invested in defining as many different ways as possible that people can be traumatized and then categorizing the post-traumatic experiences of various kinds of trauma. This cataloging includes the predisposing vulnerabilities and resilience capacities of the individual as well as the fortunate and unfortunate socio-cultural circumstances following the trauma which may contribute positively or negatively to the ongoing life of the individual involved. This is essentially a public health model which attempts to generalize or average across populations for traumatic after-effects and treatment techniques. The many and varied theoretical and technical approaches to treating trauma and post-traumatic experience that have been put forth in recent years are generally based upon some specific rationale of the psychology and/or physiology of traumatic experience and some prescription as to what ameliorative measures ought to be taken—with positive results being widely reported.[5]

# Resistance to Re-experiencing Trauma

It is notable that regardless of the theoretical or technical approaches taken, all workers in the field are acutely aware of the forces of "resistance" operating in the treatment of trauma and post-traumatic experience. While forces of resistance may be formulated in many different ways, the bottom line of the discussion is that none of us gracefully re-arranges habits in our psychological, somatic, or relational lives without grief and/or growing pains of one sort or another. "No pain, no gain" is as true for growing our minds as it is for growing and strengthening our bodies and our relationships. We know that physical and mental strength as well as determined commitment and available resources (time, money, and the skill sets of the therapeutic other) are all key factors in promoting significant and lasting change—in our present concern, the change required to overcome the debilitating effects of cumulative developmental trauma.

From the vantage point of Interpersonal/Relational Psychotherapy a key *resistance* is the tendency to feel personally—with cultural support—a victim to traumatic narratives and moments rather than *to search for ways of taking personal responsibility for the internal experience that we are retaining as a habit in the aftermath.*

The *therapeutic* questions are: "Yes a blow landed, *but how did I respond to it?* What did *I* arrange or re-arrange in my inner life in order to deal with the blow and to respond the way I did? What were the prior forces in my life that determined my choice of reactions? And how do the effects of *my* responses linger on in my mind, body, and relationships? What can *I* re-arrange *within myself today* to get past these debilitating effects?"

## Reality: The Therapist's Dilemma

Through years of training psychotherapists my number one difficulty has been how to encourage therapists to relinquish or loosen their hold on their own personally created realities in order to join their clients in discovering and unraveling the mysteries of *their* realities. That is, we each are born into a family with its own realities and every person in this family teaches us something new to add to our personal sense of what is to be counted as good and real and what is to be unseen, unwanted, and dissociated as bad, non-existent, or to be avoided. As we grow into the broader socio-cultural-linguistic community we are further introduced into other constructed realities. Yet later as therapists our education into professional life teaches us even more complex clinical and theoretical "realities."[6]

As developing human beings we grow into accepting various kinds of constructed realities and value systems that are offered to us along the way. Then we grow into creatively constructing our own sense of who we are, how we are to be, and how the people and the world around us are or should be. That is, we develop our own identity, life story and personal corner on reality.

The question for a therapist in training or for a therapist on a new, more "in-depth" or "relational" career trajectory, is how to de-center from previously learned realities in order to be available to engage with clients in studying the determining effects of their own highly idiosyncratic internalized relational traumas in the present moment. That is, how do we set aside as much as possible our own painfully learned and constructed views of the world so that we are available to enter into a dynamic relational understanding of the subjective internal and interpersonally constructed worlds of others? It is our task as therapists to listen—in the broadest possible sense of the word—carefully to others and to the ways that they have constructed their own unique worlds of experience and the ways they engage us in them. Further, there is an even more advanced step of listening not only to what is being consciously communicated to us, and not only to what is being affectively and unconsciously communicated to us, but listening in the moment to ourselves in our depths listening to our clients. Also, it is possible for any two people engaged in a committed intimate relationship to de-center from their own realities enough to experience the subjective reality of their partners. The British psychoanalyst Wilfred Bion (1992) advises listening, "without memory or desire", that is, staying with what is happening in the relationship moment by moment without having an agenda from the past or for the future—a difficult feat to accomplish, but one that is helpful in allowing traumatic experiences to emerge in the here-and-now relatedness of the therapeutic encounter. Bion is an advocate of our paying close attention to our somatic sensations and to our reveries for clues as to what may be being communicated or experienced in other invisible realms of the relationship.

How and to what extent can each of us struggle towards relinquishing our own personal hold on our constructed realities in order to immerse ourselves in *re-living* with others their personally constructed realities? This question becomes particularly acute when we imagine trying to witness empathically another person re-experiencing traumas from their personal past—and in so doing *engaging us in that re-living through transference and countertransference re-experiencing of the helplessness and terror of the trauma*. A stunning example of this de-centering process comes from fiction.[7]

## De-centering from Our Own Subjectivity: Barbara Kingsolver

From outside of my privately constructed world, a psychologist might speak of my character or my personality as an *object* for observation—like, "He is self-centered and narcissistic." But if she wants to grasp what *my particular world of experience* means, that psychologist will have to "de-center" from her own subjective world where I am an object to her and try to grasp *what my subjective world is like for me and what that is like for her*. Learning how to de-center from one's personal way of seeing others and to experience others intersubjectivity is the chief skill of a psychotherapist—but it can be practiced by anyone.

People speak of a therapist ideally as being "nonjudgmental," but this misses the point entirely. A therapist may be highly judgmental, and for good reasons. The question is rather, can the therapist, or the person who desires intimacy, momentarily suspend or loosen the hold on her own subjective position enough to grasp some of the subjective emotional realities of her relating partner and how those affect her? For example, can a therapist set aside personal and cultural attitudes toward addictive behaviors as merely "escapes," "substitutes," or "self-destructive," and join with the subjective sense of the other person who takes delight in the addictive experience and the good sense of well-being that it momentarily offers—and whatever that may mean to him past, present, and future. That would be de-centering for the purpose of making genuine emotional contact with another person.

Barbara Kingsolver in her novel *Animal Dreams* has a passage illustrating the de-centering process. The heroine, Codi, struggles with her disapproval of her Navajo boyfriend Loyd's passion for cockfighting. She struggles to de-center from her own distaste in order to understand what cockfighting means to him and yet let him know how deeply disturbed she is by his aggressive passion.

Loyd Persmooth was called up next. A rooster was delivered

into his arms, smooth as a loaf of bread, as he made his way down to the pit. This time I watched. I owed him that.

In the first fight I'd watched birds, but this time I watched Loyd, and soon understood that in this unapologetically brutal sport there was a vast tenderness between the handler and his bird. Loyd cradled this rooster in his arms, stroking and talking to it in a low, steady voice. At the end, he blew his own breath into its mouth to inflate a punctured lung. He did this when the bird was nigh unto death and clearly unable to win. The physical relationship between Loyd and his rooster transcended winning or losing.

It lasted up to the moment of death, and not one second longer. I shivered as he tossed the feathered corpse, limp as cloth, into the back of the truck. The thought of Loyd's hands on me made the skin of my forearms recoil from my own touch. [Later, going home in the truck I asked Loyd,]

'What do they do with the dead birds?' I wanted to know.
'What?'

'What do they do with them? Does somebody eat them? *Arroz con pollo*?'

He laughed. 'Not here. In Mexico I've heard they do.'...

'What do they do with them here?'

'Why, you hungry?'

'I'm asking a question.'

'There's a dump, down that arroyo a ways. A big pit. They bury them in a mass grave. Tomb of the unknown chicken.'

I ignored his joke. 'I think I'd feel better about the whole thing if the chickens were being eaten.'

'The meat'd be tough,' Loyd said, amused. He was in a good mood. He'd lost his first fight but had won four more after that—more than anyone else that day.

'It just seems like such a pathetic waste. All the time and effort that goes into those chicken's lives, from the hatched egg to the grave of the unknown chicken. Pretty pointless.' I needed to make myself clear. 'No, it's not pointless. It's pointed in a direction that makes me uncomfortable.'

'Those roosters don't know what's happening to them. You think a fighting cock thinks its life is pointless?'

'No, I think a fighting cock is stupider than a head of lettuce.' I glanced at Loyd, hoping he'd be hurt by my assessment, but apparently he agreed. I wanted him to defend his roosters. It frightened me that he could connect so intensely with a bird and then, in a breath, disengage.

'It's a clean sport,' he said. 'It might be hard to understand, for an outsider, but it's something I grew up with. You don't see drunks, and the betting is just a very small part of it. The crowd is nicer than at a football game.'

'I don't disagree with any of that.'

'It's a skill you have in your hands. You can go anywhere pick up any bird, even one that's not your own, a bird you've never seen before, and you can do this thing with it.'

'Like playing the piano,' I said.

'Like that,' he said, without irony.

'I could see that you're good at it. Very good.' I struggled to find my point, but could come up only with disturbing, disjointed images: A woman in the emergency room on my first night of residency, stabbed eighteen times by her lover. Curty and Glen sitting in the driveway dappled with rooster blood. Hallie in a jeep, hitting a land mine. Those three girls.

'Everything dies, Codi.'

'Oh, great. Tell me something I don't know. My mother died when I was a three-year-old baby!' I had no idea where that came from. I looked out the window and wiped my eyes carefully with my sleeve. But the tears kept coming. For a long time I cried for those three teenage girls who were split apart from above while they picked fruit. For the first time I really believed in my heart it had happened. That someone could look down, aim a sight, pull a trigger. Feel nothing. Forget.

Loyd seemed at a loss. Finally he said gently, 'I mean animals die. They suffer in nature and they suffer in the barnyard. It's not like people. They weren't meant to live a good life and then go to heaven, or wherever we go.'

As plainly as anything then, I remembered trying to save the coyotes from the flood. My ears filled with the roars of the flooded river and my nose with the strong stench of mud. I gripped the armrest of Loyd's truck to keep the memory from drowning my senses. I heard my own high voice commanding Hallie to stay with me. And then, later, asking Doc Homer, 'Will they go to heaven?' I couldn't

35

hear his answer, probably because he didn't have one. I hadn't wanted facts, I'd wanted salvation.

Carefully, so as not to lose anything, I brought myself back to the present and sat still, paying attention. 'I'm not talking about chicken souls. I don't believe chickens have souls,' I said slowly. 'What I believe is that humans should have more heart than that. I can't feel good about people making a spectator sport out of puncture wounds and internal hemorrhage.'

Loyd kept his eyes on the dark air above the road. Bugs swirled in the headlights like planets cut loose from their orbits, doomed to chaos. After a full half hour he said, 'My brother Leander got killed by a drunk, about fifteen miles from here.'

In another half hour he said, 'I'll quit, Codi. I'm quitting right now.'[8]

We see in this conversation how hard two people work to de-center from their own personal orientation to appreciate the other's internal world of emotional experience. Further, Kingsolver shows us how relational experiences from the past of each character come to bear on the present relatedness moment. It is as if a third person is present in the relationship as each of them struggles to hold their own subjective position, while simultaneously de-centering and appreciating the subjective position of the other. In their conversation and in the hour of silence during the nighttime truck ride, we feel the mutual transformation (the transformation in "O"). taking place as each relinquishes the fixedness of their own subjective worlds and resonates emotionally with the other's—"Loyd kept his eyes on the dark air above the road. Bugs swirled in the headlights like planets cut loose from their orbits, doomed to chaos." And chaos it does so often seem as we relinquish hard-won emotional footing and attempt to join subjective worlds with another—but through this process the mysterious and invisible third person of the therapeutic process emerges.[9]

If you and I engage in a conversation and we each try to grasp the other person's points of view—the inner subjective experiences of the other—then we must momentarily abandon our centeredness in our own worlds and attempt to recognize each other's points of view, opinions, feelings, and personal orientations. That is, we must for the moment step away from the security of our own subjective worlds in order to experience each other's.

Psychologists speak of this process of mutually engaging each other's subjective worlds as a process of "intersubjectivity." This de-centering process differs sharply from my simply trying to understand you as an object from within my subjective point of view. This de-centering process differs from various attempts to "improve communication" or "work out compromises" in relationships.

I realize that "subjectivity" and "intersubjectivity" are technical concepts developed in psychology, but if we are to experience intimacy to its fullest extent, we need meaningful vocabulary to consider how minds can emotionally penetrate to the "inside" of each other on a regular basis. The "mirroring mechanisms" recently discovered in neurobiology add substance to our ability to live momentarily at the other person's center.[1] These concepts allow us a way of thinking and speaking about the emotional encounters necessarily involved in intensifying human intimacy and encountering our own and our relating partner's cumulative relational traumas. Further, as we will later see, Interpersonal/Relational Psychotherapy demonstrates that it is highly useful to personify the intersubjective field as the third person, so that we can learn to listen when it "speaks" to us about ourselves and our relationships in various ways.[10]

Interpersonal/Relational psychology now holds that the human mind is not simply a function of an isolated brain existing in between the ears of individuals. Rather, mind is conceived of a complex communal phenomenon existing between and among individual organisms—not only of our species but among all species since the beginning of time. Interpersonal/Relational Psychotherapy is committed to studying the human processes of subjectivity, intersubjectivity, and the third force (personified as the "third person") involved in the complexities of intimate human relationships.

# Some Imprecise Definitions

While "trauma" has been defined and redefined many times according to different points of view, the bottom-line definition always goes back to Freud who spoke of the traumatic situation as a moment when the person's ego (sense of "I" or sense of self) is so overwhelmed by intrusive stimulation that it cannot comfortably or effectively process what is happening at the time (Freud 1933). The overwhelmed or overstimulated ego/self here is understood to be the fetus', neonate's, infant's, child's, or adult's personally constructed

38

habits of being in the world that, due to internal or external stimulation are strained, stretched, or collapsed to the point that some accommodative defensive response is required to shore up an otherwise helplessly disintegrating self in the throes of confusion, panic and terror. Note again here that the accent is on understanding *the person's internal response to the stimulation* rather than to the overstimulating or intrusive event itself.

"Dissociation" has in the past often been thought of as the ego's or self's (pathological, defensive) response to a traumatic intrusion. The idea has been that when the total span of the ego operative at the moment could not tolerate the overstimulation, a part of the ego would become split or separated off into a different dissociated "self-structure" or "self-state" (A. Freud 1937).

More recently as the Interpersonal/Relational perspective in psychotherapy has emerged, dissociation has come to be understood differently as a universal and essentially normal developmental process. In this understanding, multiple, affectively-tinged self-states are thought to be present from before birth and to operate in various relational contexts. For example, one relational self-state exists in the presence of a satisfying breast while different self-state exists in the presence of a frustrating breast. With favorable development through good-enough parenting these many self-states tend to be gradually brought under the umbrella of a central unified sense of self—but multiple self-states are always potentially present waiting to be called out in an intersubjective relational moment.)

Considered in this manner, an expectable reaction to the ego's current integration being disturbed by excessive stimulation would be to shift, to retreat or to "dissociate" into one or several already formed self-states. That is, rather than the assumption of a unitary self from birth with parts being defensively split off due to traumatic blows, the Interpersonal/Relational view holds that multiple self-states are present from before birth and potentially present throughout a lifetime and subject to being dissociatively reawakened in various relational situations.

The interpersonal/relational psychotherapy literature now abounds with clinical examples wherein both client and therapist during moments of intense interaction demonstrate dissociative processes as normative events in response to intensely stimulating intimate engagements (Bromberg 1998, 2008, 2011; Stern 2003, 2010, 2013; Benjamin 2010, 2004, 2013; Davies 1996, 1999, 2006 ; Aron 1991, 2001; Hedges 1992, 1994a, 1994c, 1996, 2000b, 2005, 2011, 2013f). Interpersonal psychiatrist Harry Stack Sullivan (1953) first described the dissociative split between the "good me", the "bad me", and the "not-me". These are simple but handy terms to describe the parts of me that I am pleased with, the parts of me that I know about but I'm not pleased with, and the parts of me that I have chosen through my history of dissociating not to accept as a part of me — though from time to time I am abruptly confronted with responses in myself that I do not wish to or cannot own as belonging to me. I mention this simplified Sullivanian conceptualization in order to illustrate how dissociation may operate in a relational context — how a dissociated not-me self-state may suddenly appear unbidden that either I or my relating partner, or both of us may be forced to deal with. At this point in our psychological history, we realize that there are an infinite number of potential me's with different affective colorings that become elicited in different relational contexts.

The terms "primary trauma" and "secondary trauma" have been used in different ways by different researchers but I will here follow the usage of Shubs (in press). In keeping with the contemporary Interpersonal/Relational psychotherapy slant on multiple (dissociated) self-states as being the universal normative condition of infancy and later life, it stands to reason that many of those self-states generated in relational contexts are ones produced by traumatically overstimulating moments brought about by events as simple as a child being moved when she doesn't want to be moved or an intractable teething pain or fever that she unrealistically expects mother to soothe. Or possibly brought about by much more intense abusive and/or intrusive stimulation. Self-states generated by normal or not so normal "primary" developmental traumas may be relegated to the realm of bad me or not-me and thus remain invisible or unknown until a later in life incident or "secondary trauma" re-activates these earlier developmental traumatic self-states. I will later tell you how I observed traumas stimulated by 9/11 events (secondary trauma) trigger countless primary traumas from early childhood in different people.

As Shubs (in press) and other somatic and psychodynamic relational therapists are quick to point out, simply addressing the current or secondary trauma—that is, the focal or the narrational event or the post-traumatic symptoms—does not get to the bottom of the matter. In practice, however, the choice of simply treating the current incident or troubling traumatic symptoms as opposed to working on unraveling prior primary traumas in an intimate safe relationship may be a matter of limited resources being available, various resistances being operative, and/or the skill sets and preferences of the listening partner being limited

*[handwritten notes in margin:]*
self-states
good me - parts I like
bad me - know but don't like
not me - dissociated
not accepted

41

# Some Ordinary People

I offer the following vignette to illustrate the way relational therapy with a couple has helped them distinguish between some of the primary and secondary traumas in their lives.

Joan and Matt sought me out when they were considering having a second child—this time with a surrogate mother. Because of necessary radiation and a hysterectomy following the aftermath of breast cancer, doctors recommended that they freeze some fertilized eggs while they still could in case they ever wanted more children—which they did.

They are a strikingly good-looking couple who are highly intelligent, thoughtful, mutually respectful and very much in love. In the beginning there had been extremely strong chemistry between them and their marriage started off wonderfully. Their now three-and-a- half-year-old son, Sean, is developing well and both parents are invested in Sean's physical and emotional care. Unfortunately, in all of the trauma they have endured with the recurring cancer and the odds of treatment failure, emotional distance slowly developed between them and sexual intimacy came to a complete stand-still— much to their mutual distress.

They want another child and a friend has offered to be the surrogate mother. New drugs have provided a "total cure" for the cancer but due to the exact nature of the cancer there will be a lifetime of medications required. Joan is justifiably proud of her courageous fight and her sense of victory over the disease. Matt admires her achievements but is very much afraid for her, for himself, and for Sean should there be a recurrence—they are not past the five- year safety mark yet.

Joan is frightened because when she was so overwhelmed with her treatment regimen there were times when she experienced Matt's emotionally withdrawing and times when his preoccupations with work left the burden of household and child-rearing responsibilities to her. Will this happen again if they undertake having a second child? Matt reluctantly admits that this indeed did happen and that emotional withdrawal in response to stress is a lifelong pattern for him, dating to severe emotional and physical abuse from his parents, especially his father.

Now is the right time to have a baby—the eggs are there, the surrogate is ready, the cure is in effect, Sean is of an age a sibling would be good, they want another child...but...? Both Joan and Matt are frozen with desire and fear—towards each other, toward the relationship, and toward the possibility of family expansion. Could I help them decide what to do and how to do it? After all this trauma how can they get back to their loving intimate relationship that they enjoyed so much? How can they be assured of a satisfying and enduring future family life?

Oh, the life of a psychotherapist! Just when we think we know what we're doing, just when we think we know how to help people with their problems—along comes something new that we have no idea whatsoever how to deal with! I said I wasn't sure how or if I might be able to help them—especially since they had already been to two counselors who turned out not to be of much help. But let's meet for a few sessions and see if we can get a conversation going that might be useful. I had no idea what that might look like.

Joan and Matt each wanted to tell me something about their families of origin and how each other's in-laws affected them. They were overjoyed to share their child-rearing experiences of Sean with

43

me and I did some coaching around some issues that were coming up at pre-school lately. Unaccountably, Sean was being more aggressive with other children and had had a few accidents in his pants lately. We talked about how sensitive young kids are to stresses parents are experiencing and to conflicts that naturally arise when parents are considering more children that will change the love structure that exists in the family.

After several sessions in which we three had established some basic comfort with each other, Joan let out a string of discontents about Matt's emotionally withdrawn behaviors, trying her best to be understanding and not critical—but she was now recovered and wanted a restoration of their former interactions and intimacy. Matt did some tearful work on his knee-jerk emotional withdrawals and re-arranged his professional work to be more present for Joan and Sean. He pledged not to let work get in the way of his family again and took some effective steps to make sure this would be so. But his sex simply wasn't working since all of this began, and he hated to begin something only to disappoint her and to feel humiliated himself. He's always been quite potent but now he has no sexual desire at all for her or anybody else, he doesn't even masturbate. She's impatient. He's apologetic. They love each other. Neither wants to break up. They're in a pickle.

As the weeks passed by Joan relates a childhood of non-recognition by her parents and her having developed a strong, aggressive, no-nonsense, self-sufficient attitude toward life and problem solving. She had become a highly successful business woman with her own thriving firm and a number of competent employees to help her run it. Matt's being soundly criticized and squelched by both parents throughout childhood left him with less than full ambition at several unsatisfying jobs until he found his present work which was exhilarating, but time and energy consuming.

I had several times posed the question to Joan of what it had been like for her after she was diagnosed and while she was going through protracted painful treatments. I got inspirational answers of how she had always put faith in herself, how she was determined, how good it felt to know she was on top of things, and a plethora of details about doctors, medications, procedures, etc.

Then came the night of trauma revisited. Joan got caught by one of my questions and her voice started cracking, she had never intended to say this to anyone, ever—and she started shaking and sobbing uncontrollably relating the utter helplessness, hopelessness, aloneness, and defeat she had experienced repeatedly during the whole ordeal—feelings she was too ashamed to tell anyone, even Matthew. She had always been ashamed of any vulnerability and had worked a lifetime to cover up any sign of weakness or insecurity. Needless to say, both Matt and I were deeply moved with compassion to witness Joan's drop into traumatic re-experiencing before our very eyes. We were relieved and pleased that Joan at last could speak her truth—like some sort of boil was popping. We all three understood that this deep emotional outpouring wasn't just about the cancer (i.e., the secondary trauma) but about her whole life of emotional aloneness, struggle, and determination to get on top of overwhelming circumstances no matter what (i.e., cumulative primary traumas). And on top her terror of failure and humiliation. In the case of the cancer she had had to surrender to humiliating defeat by a powerful force greater than herself. But her good old spirit of determination did kick in like it always did and she had achieved the best possible outcome.

In response, the following week Matt dropped into his own shaking and sobbing and the humiliation and defeat he had suffered repeatedly as a child from his abusive parents and how the only place that was safe was to hide, to become emotionally withdrawn, isolated and invisible but terribly alone. He had found Joan and for the first time in his life had a safe companion until the diagnosis when he found himself re-traumatized and once again very much alone with the prospects of losing her. Matt knows she's "cured" but he's terrified something else might happen and he'll be all alone with two children and no support. The cancer experience had thrown him back to a terrible sense of failure and a lack of confidence in himself. Joan and I resonated deeply with his life-long trauma and fear of more re-traumatization and failure.

From this brief account we can see that Joan and Matthew were hell-bent on doing the work they had to do to come clean with themselves and with each other about how the cancer trauma (i.e., the sets of secondary traumas) had affected them. They needed to know for themselves and for each other how this life circumstance tapped into the worst of their growing up experiences and how as children they had each learned to close off to fear of defeat, aloneness, and shame — she by active, aggressive, competence and he by withdrawal and isolation (i.e., their primary traumas).

The following sessions featured a cascade of painful childhood memories and more elucidation of the fears they were experiencing in their present life situation. How were they going to get things back together? How could they ever feel safe in love again? And if they couldn't restore the intimacy of their marital relationship how were they going to be good parents? Should they risk having another child?

I end the story here, with my main point about the importance of breaking through the current or secondary trauma to re-*experience* the original or primary traumas in order to establish more truth and intimacy in the present relational situation having been made. This brief story also illustrates *the importance of experiencing a retraumatization in the here-and-now with committed and emotionally involved others*.

Joan and Matt were so relieved to restore honesty and to be once again working together as a team that, even with much relationship work yet to accomplish in order to regain lost territory, they felt confident to go ahead with having another child—hopefully this time a girl, but another boy would be great too!

We all know this experience. Some life circumstance traumatically triggers an emotional overload that needs to be ventilated with a relating partner. Usually when the conversation begins neither has the slightest idea what is about to happen but both sense some kind of highly-charged pressure present. And then, almost without warning something starts to erupt—a deep energy impelling the overloaded person forward. It may start with an outpouring of frustration or rage over the realities of the triggering situation (secondary trauma). But comes the emotional eruption and both people know something much greater is at stake, that something deep is emerging in the rapid-fire jumbled and irrational thoughts that tumble out. "Thank God this is private and confidential—I'm so humiliated and ashamed at what I'm saying, I don't even know if it's all true, but it seems important. I'm so confused, I don't even know where all of this is coming from." A good listener remains low-key but facilitating and encouraging. "Keep going. No you're not upsetting me. No it doesn't yet all make sense but let it fly! You have to get this out. You have to get to the bottom of whatever's happening for you." And then the cascade of jumbled memories of similar past horrors and frustrations and how helpless, alone, frightened and defeated we felt at those times and in those circumstances (primary traumas). "Now what's going on for me in the present begins to make more sense." This sense of trauma isn't about just now but about a lifetime of similar traumatic humiliations. And so it goes.

The most important and relieving experiences of our lives have proceeded this way with someone we trusted or needed to trust with our burden. Often, for example in therapy, it goes on for long periods of time with someone to witness our actual re-living in the present the dreadful cumulative traumatic experiences of the past.

If you happen to be one of those rare people who has never trusted enough to open up deep pockets of emotional trauma from the past for re-experiencing with someone you can trust in the present, then you of all people probably are in sore need of doing so. As I hope to demonstrate in this book, we all have a history of traumatic moments that we have handled in various ways and then done our best to cover up and move on. The dissociations run deep. But the inhibitions necessarily involved in emotional and physical trauma and dissociation none-the-less live on in our minds and bodies with ominous consequences for our health, wellbeing, and longevity.

On a final note I had the listener above saying "No, this isn't disturbing me." Of course, many times this is not true and only the truth should be spoken. In fact, as I will demonstrate later, as the therapy deepens the therapist is rarely personally okay with what's happening. The primitive and dissociative experiences of the client necessarily impinge upon the therapist's own psychological functioning and well-being and the two together often have to struggle through mutual dissociations and enactments as well as mutual "chase and dodge" as well as "rupture and repair" experiences in order to experience the deep work of trauma recovery.[11]

*Part Two*
# Developmental Fears and Cumulative Trauma

## Cumulative Developmental Trauma

The concept of "cumulative strain trauma" was first put forward by psychoanalyst Masud Khan in 1962. He noted that certain babies were born into relational environments which simply did not match well their native dispositions, a situation that resulted in constant strained traumatic adaptations between caregiver and infant or child. He took the position, that has since been confirmed many times over, that cumulative strain trauma can be as disastrous for child development as various kinds of more focal or event traumas.

Fifty years later as we gradually realize that repeated traumas throughout the growing up years and into adulthood are not only normal and expectable but necessary for robust development, we can return to Khan's thinking and realize that the effects of normal developmental traumas are also cumulative over time. Further, it is now widely recognized that relational patterns that are internalized early in development profoundly affect how a child or adult perceives and experiences later traumatic relational impingements. The therapeutic implications of this are clear: Every traumatic experience of later life is received and experienced through perceptual lenses and adaptational patterns established earlier in life. In fact, it becomes useful to conceptualize a cascading effect wherein an early pattern of trauma adaptation determines the nature and quality of a later one and both determine yet later ones and so on down the line into the inevitable traumas of old age and dying.

When attempting to sort through the effects of trauma it is helpful to have a map of the universal relational challenges that humans can experience as overwhelming and frightening. Over a century of psychoanalytic study seven watersheds of human development have emerged as general relational situations that can—through fear—lead to significant mental constrictions and physical contractions. I've chosen to refer to these universal relational fears as "Seven Deadly Fears" as our retention of their effects can prove unhealthy and even life-threatening.

When investigators and therapists from the trauma community seek to isolate the facts and narratives of the trauma currently being presented for relief it seems their treatment tactics rarely recognize that what's going on now necessarily has an adaptational history reaching back to infancy—that one traumatic adaptation is laid on top of another creating a complex cumulative experiential situation. Nor do their treatment strategies often include the awareness *that it is not remembering or abreacting to the trauma per se that is therapeutically decisive, but rather the re-experiencing of the cumulative patterns repeatedly in the here-and-now transference, resistance, and countertransference dimensions of the therapeutic relationship itself.[12]* This tendency was well-illustrated during the mid-1990's "recovered memory" fiasco that set off an international epidemic of "false memory syndrome" until courts and professional ethics codes firmly curtailed the movement. While I cannot here fully explicate the problem as I did in an earlier book (1994c), the bottom line is that it is easier for two people to resist the hard work of living and working through the here-and-now relational remembering patterns than it is to jointly search for the set of traumatic facts and narrations "out there and back then."[13] *Interpersonal/Relational Psychotherapy seeks to establish a secure and safe long-term, interpersonal, intersubjective relationship in which the history of cumulative developmental traumas can emerge at their own pace and in their own way in here-and-now experiencing and working through processes that can provide personality transformations that allow much more than mere relief of the presenting symptoms.*

# Listening to Cascading Traumatic Experiences: September 11, 2001

Over forty years as a practicing psychotherapist and psychoanalyst experiencing my own clients and myself working through traumatic experiences and serving as a consultant to literally hundreds of therapists in Southern California and elsewhere dealing with traumatic experiences they and their clients are experiencing, I can safely say that the cascading effects of cumulative developmental trauma manifest at every turn. The most telling of these cases are reported in a series of books produced under my authorship by therapists at the Listening Perspectives Study Center and the Newport Psychoanalytic Institute located in Orange County, California (Hedges 1983, 1992, 1994a,b,c, 1996, 2000a,b, 2005, 2013e).

But the events that stand out in my memory as illustrating most clearly how current traumas trigger previous traumas happened in wake of the 9/11 disaster. I have told the story in my free download book, *Overcoming Relationship Fears* (2013c) and have summarized it in the accompanying *Workbook for Overcoming Relationship Fears* (2013d). Here's my version of those events.

On Tuesday morning September 11, 2001 my daughter Breta called in frantic, heaving sobs to tell me of the terrorist attack on the World Trade Center. Telephone gripped in hand, I raced to the TV in time to witness live the second tower hit and to hear Breta's terrified screaming through the receiver. Not only was I stricken by what I was witnessing on the television, but I was paralyzed with another kind of fear—the fear of being utterly helpless, of being completely unable to do anything to buffer the terror that was shattering my beloved daughter. I yearned to hold Breta, to take her into my arms and quell the fear like when she was a little girl with the forest next to our home going up in giant flames—I held her tightly then, both of us shaking in helpless horror watching the fire fighters struggling to quench the blaze threatening to destroy our home.

But on 9/11 I was utterly helpless—there was absolutely nothing I could to do to restore the World Trade Center or my daughter's fragmenting sense of safety and peace of mind—nor my own.

We all experienced the paralyzing effects of fear on that fateful day—eyes wide open, hearts racing, lungs tight, guts wrenched, muscles tight, and a total body weakness and body-mind numbness that lasted for weeks and that will never leave us completely.

In the wake of the attack one of my therapy clients spent two days curled up in the bottom of her closet, like she used to as a small child after her alcoholic father had abused her. Another client re-lived a tragic teenage freeway accident in which his four closest friends had been instantly killed while he, the driver and sole survivor, had lived on in helpless loneliness and guilt. One woman re-agonized the prolonged cancer death of her mother when she was four years old, remembering feeling that her bad behavior was killing her mother. After 9/11 she had again heard her mother's screams of intractable pain and terror of dying. No matter how good she was, no matter how hard she tried, it was not enough to keep mother from leaving her forever.

I asked each client the week of 9/11 where the attack had taken them. Everyone recalled horrifying memories from earlier in life that had resurfaced in response to that terrible moment. When asked where in their bodies they were feeling the pain, the agony, the terror—everyone knew exactly what parts of their body had taken the hit. Some had chest or abdominal pain, others had headaches, tight jaws, back pain, joint pains, asthma attacks, muscle spasms, or whatever—the list went on.

What became absolutely clear to me after 9/11 was that each of us has our own unique ways of experiencing fear. And that our individual patterns of fear live on as destructive hangovers from childhood relationship experiences to impact our minds and bodies in highly specific ways.

People in therapy had long ago shown me how childhood trauma interferes with later intimate relationships. But the 9/11 terrorist attacks revealed that all of us have deeply buried personal patterns of fear left over from earlier experiences that can be reactivated on a moment's notice—relationship fears that are physical as well as mental.

Airplanes being down, I made the 12-hour drive to Albuquerque to keep my Saturday speaking commitment with the New Mexico Psychoanalytic Society on my new book, *Terrifying Transferences: Aftershocks of Childhood Trauma*. The topic could not have been more timely—we were all in aftershock. Therapists flocked in from all over the state crowding the large auditorium to talk about the shattering experiences we had just been through. We had all heard story after story of childhood trauma revisited—not to mention having our own traumatic reactions and re-experiencing our own childhood horrors.

Given the emotionally-charged circumstances that day, I opened the floor first thing in the morning for venting about our trying week. I listened carefully as therapist after therapist told of traumatic reactions they had been witness to in their consulting rooms following the Tuesday disaster.

As I listened to the stories therapists told that day, one more critical thing about fear and trauma emerged—we have more power over our fears than we think! We have the power to re-experience past traumas and to get some resolution in the context of current safe and intimate relationships. The New Mexico therapists were well-experienced in how to intervene to help people re-experience long-buried fear reactions being revived in the present. They knew how to encourage people to tell stories, to create pictures and to tune into body reactions from the past that had been stimulated by the terrifying events in the present. The New Mexico therapists told me how, depending on each client's unique fears and physical reactions, they were able to show their clients how to release the terrifying grip that habitual fear holds over mind, body, and relationship. Some people needed to be encouraged to breathe deeply while remembering some long-forgotten horror. Others needed to sob, to rage, to pace the room, to lie on the floor in numbed silence, to hold hands, to hug, to pray.

The realities of 9/11 were bad enough to have to experience as a current reality, but the human tendency to layer new realities on top of old unresolved past terrors was making life utterly unbearable for clients and therapists alike that week. An enlightened therapeutic approach had much release and relief to offer. The New Mexico conference room was electrified that day as we shared our week's experiences and as therapists allowed themselves an opportunity to rage, to sigh, to sob or to cringe in helpless fear. Who could imagine what might happen next?

What I had learned that week in my consulting room and that day with the New Mexico therapists had to be shared with others. I had to find a way to show people how our individual childhood patterns of fear live on in our minds and bodies ready to be reactivated in response to impacting experiences at any time. And that our long-established fear reflexes are deeply enmeshed in our body-mind-relationship (BMR) selves.

Clients I've worked with over the years had taught me about the kinds of early relational experiences that children find frightening. Body workers and health professionals who specialize in locating and releasing body tensions had taught me how to tune into our moment-by-moment somatic experiences. The New Mexico therapists made clear to me how we can put those hangover fear reflexes into stories, pictures, memories, and body sensations that can be emotionally re-experienced in a present intimate relationship. They clarified for me the interpersonal process required to release ourselves from the paralyzing effects of longstanding patterns of mental anguish and physical fear. That is, long-standing fears can be encouraged to re-emerge in an intimate relationship setting. When two emotionally involved people experience together long-suppressed trauma there is hope of at last finding ways to release the grip that fear has over our body-mind-relationship (BMR) connections.

When Breta and I got together the week after 9/11, we re-experienced the frightening fire that affected us both when she was three years old, a frightening car accident that we were involved in when she was seven, and a number of other frightening circumstances from both of our lives. Her mother and I had separated just before Breta turned three. Judy and I had both maintained a close parenting relationship with Breta throughout her growing up years so that sharing emotional experiences together had always been a part of our lives. Breta and I certainly found our sharing our 9/11 experience, and all that it brought up for us, to be both relieving and integrating.

My experiences with Breta on 9/11 and with the New Mexico psychoanalysts and psychotherapists shortly after illustrate what we already know about fear—that it is a *body-mind-relationship* experience. Connecting to our deepest selves is a matter of locating our body-mind-relationship connection. For convenience, a new term emerges, *the BMR connection* (pronounced "Beam-er"). I will use the term BMR connection to designate that central place in our selves where body, mind, and relationship are one. Once you get used to thinking in terms of your BMR connections you will find the term useful shorthand. It is helpful to think of a deep-seated body-mind-relationship connection that instinctively contracts in reflexive response to intrusive stimulation. The particular and idiosyncratic body-mind-relationship contraction is held in memory and predetermines later reactions to traumatic intrusions. Needless to say, chronically held contractions threaten well-being and longevity.

If we want to understand the impact our BMR fear reflexes have on us, it helps to have a general map of the kinds of fears that are common to all people. The Seven Deadly Fears that I will elaborate arise from seven kinds of complex relationship challenges that we each had to contend with in the course of growing up. There are, of course, many specific things that we are each individually afraid of. But the seven developmental relationship challenges give rise to relational fears in all people.

Most of us have lived a lifetime with low-grade daily tensions of various kinds that continue to sap our energy and to limit our relational flexibility. Learning to contact and then to release our fear reflexes is finally a matter of slowly pushing ourselves into painful areas of background tension—first in our bodies and then into the frightening words, sensations, and images that emerge in our BMR connection. *Since human fear reflexes are not developed in the jungle as with most mammals, but rather in the confines of intimate human relationships, our habitual fear reflexes can best be re-experienced in actual here-and-now intimate human relationships.* Interpersonal/Relational Psychotherapy has been devised to do just that—to set up ongoing interpersonal exchanges in which a cascade of fear reflexes memorializing traumatic moments of the past can come into play and can be worked on together in the here-and-now therapeutic relationship.

# Overcoming Our Relational Fears: An Overview

Following the 9/11 disaster I had occasion to re-think the four

Listening Perspectives previously used in Interpersonal/Relational Psychotherapy in terms of fear and how fears resulting from primary traumas reside in our bodies and our relationships to determine how each of us experience later secondary traumas. The result became the book *Overcoming Our Relational Fears* (2013d) with a companion *Overcoming Our Relational Fears Workbook* (2013e) of exercises for individuals or couples designed to locate where in their bodies and relationships their primary traumas reside (both books are free downloads from the International Psychotherapy Institute's website, freepsychotherapybooks.org).

---

# Considering Seven Universal Developmental Fears[14]

We are all aware that chronic tension saps our energy and contributes to such modern maladies as chronic fatigue, fibromyalgia and high blood pressure, but few of us realize that these are caused by muscle constrictions that started as relationship fears in early childhood and live on in our minds and bodies. These early traumatic responses become fear reflexes that create habitual reactions to the challenges of everyday life and can cripple our relationship experiences at all developmental levels. Over time they can even lead to tissue deterioration that threatens our health, well-being, and longevity. Muscle tension from unresolved emotional trauma has been the basis of therapeutic bodywork for nearly a century. What has become clear is that somatic tension often arises from childhood relationship fears. For example, if we repeatedly reached out and our caregivers didn't respond, we came to fear that our needs would never be met. When we were punished for asserting ourselves, we came to fear that the world would not allow us to be ourselves. When our ecstatic joy came into conflict with social norms, we came to fear that we couldn't live joyfully and be passionately alive.

Keying on seven universal developmental fears, in my book and workbook I show how to use them to map out our own personal body-mind-relationship (BMR) connections. Since human fear reflexes (trauma responses) were created in child-caregiver relationships, they can best be re-experienced in intimate human relating. By feeling the background tension—at first in our bodies and then in words and images—triggered by our intimate relationships, we can identify these fears, release them, and free up the blocked energy. From here we can trace each fear back and release the fear-source of other body tensions.

*Overcoming Our Relationship Fears* is a user-friendly roadmap for healing our relationships by dealing with our childhood fear reflexes. It is replete with relationship stories to illustrate each of the Seven Deadly Fears and how we individually express them. I show how to use our own built-in "Aliveness Monitor" to gauge our body's reactions to daily interactions and how they trigger our fears. Exercises in the accompanying workbook help release these life-threatening constrictions and reclaim aliveness with ourselves and others.

# The Body-Mind-Relationship (BMR) Connection

We know that fear can keep us out of harm's way, but fear can also prevent us from putting our personal truths and needs out there.

As a therapist for forty years, I have often seen how our fears based on cumulative developmental traumas limit and cripple us in many ways. But it was while swimming laps in an exercise pool and sensing muscle tension after a day of difficult relationship exchanges, that I first realized that our bodies are at all times meaningfully enmeshed in our relationships. And the most important body-mind-relationship (BMR) connection is with fear. Here are chapter summaries of *Overcoming Relationship Fears* that may point the way for therapeutic re-experiencing.

## Mapping the Seven Deadly Fears in Your BMR Connection

While we've known that fear is a body-mind-relationship experience, the key is to locate the internal connection between the effect or pain, and the cause or trauma, which I term the BMR connection. I identify *Seven Deadly Fears* that arise from relationship challenges and traumas that we all faced while growing up, and the fear reflexes they created. First, we must identify our personal body tensions or the effect of the fear. Then, since they were developed in our child-caregiver relationships, our habitual fear reflexes can best be reexperienced in our intimate human relationships and/or our therapeutic relationships.

## Dave Fights His Way Out of Fear

As an illustration, I tell a story about Dave's car-buying trauma. Dave hates buying a new car and having to haggle over price and the back-and-forth offers. One day Dave got a great car deal, but the hour-long harangue had been humiliating and intimidating. The whole ordeal created a rage in him. Analysis uncovered traumatic feelings of helplessness from reaching out as an infant and as a child and not getting acknowledged, then going into a rage before capitulating and feeling helpless. While recalling this memory on the analytic couch, Dave's feet, legs, and fists had begun violently twitching. The BMR connection had been found and Dave could work from there.

## Fear in the BMR Connection—Destructive Hangovers from the Past

Like Dave we have all developed disturbing reactions to traumatizing childhood relationship situations. Unfortunately, we suppress these fears and our awareness of them, until later in life we often can't distinguish between real dangers in the present and our habitual responses from the past. We end up asking ourselves why we experience chronic tension and pains with no apparent physical reason. It may not occur to us that we are habitually afraid of intimate relationships. The source of cumulative traumatic experience is buried in our past reaching out—from the grave, as it were—to stifle our creative expression and dampen our passionate spirits in the living present.

## Experience Your BMR Connection: Putting on Your Aliveness Monitor

In this chapter I have readers imagine slipping into a glove-tight body suit that acts as our "Aliveness Monitor." With its electronic probes and sensors, it monitors all of our bodily reactions to life situations from an accelerated heart rate to dilation of the eyes. With it we can gauge how our fear reactions appear, how long they are sustained, and how constrictions were or were not released. The good news is that our bodies already possess built-in Aliveness Monitors and if we cultivate a heightened awareness of our body tensions, we can trace them back to the fear reflex that feeds them.

## Experience Your BMR Connection: Touching Base with Your Body

Here I present a set of simple exercises that if done in the morning or at various stress points during the day connects us to our breathing and helps alert us to where in our bodies we are holding tension at the moment. Each exercise stretches various parts of the body while monitoring sensations that offer clues to where we are holding tension. As you release tension, spontaneous images and memories will emerge that point to traumatic relationship challenges—past, present, and future. These tension-identifying exercises include: 1) Breathe and Reach; 2) Open Your Chest and Release Your Shoulders; 3) Release Your Lower Back and Pelvis; 4) Ground Your legs and Feet; 5) Breathe and Reach Again.

## I Dreamed of Being Scared to Death

I next illustrate the BMR Connection with a personal story. For years I had been teaching a state-mandated day-long course in law & ethics to therapists. I was overall comfortable with the ballroom-size venues, but after each class I would feel somehow "beaten-up." After one teaching event I had a dream about discovering that the latch on an old-time gas basement furnace (like the one I grew up with) is locked from the inside, and when opening it a child's charred body falls out. In the dream I hear the child screaming for Daddy repeatedly, but father was powerless to help. This harkened back to my childhood abuse by my mother at the hands of my stern father. Then I saw the connection to my classes: by teaching a required course to "captive" therapists, I had come to anticipate being the helpless victim of their rage and resentment. No wonder I felt uptight and tense in my BMR connection at the end of the teaching day! Having now experienced and released the connection, I generally feel exhilarated at the end of a teaching day!

## Considering the Seven Deadly Fears

Next, *in the order of their increasing relational complexity*, I have provided subchapters explaining and illustrating with stories each of the *Seven Deadly Fears*. Try to take in the importance of each fear as they will be used later in each of the case illustrations.

1. **The Fear of Being Alone**: We dread reaching out and finding nobody there to respond to our needs. We fear being ignored, being left alone, and being seen as unimportant. We feel the world does not respond to our needs. So what's the use of trying?

2. **The Fear of Connecting**: Because of frightening and painful experiences in the past, connecting emotionally and intimately with others feels dangerous. Our life experiences have left us feeling that the world is not a safe place. We fear injury so we withdraw from emotionally intimate connections.

3. **The Fear of Being Abandoned**: After having connected emotionally or bonded with someone, we fear being either abandoned with our own needs or being swallowed up by the other person's. In either case, we feel the world is not a dependable place, that we live in danger of emotional

64

abandonment. We may become clingy and dependent, or we may become super-independent—or both.

4.  **The Fear of Self-Assertion**: We have all experienced rejection, and perhaps even punishment for expressing ourselves in a way that others don't like. We thus may learn to fear asserting ourselves and letting our needs be known in relationships. We feel the world does not allow us to be truly ourselves. We may either cease putting ourselves out there altogether, or may assert ourselves with demanding vengeance.

5.  **The Fear of Lack of Recognition**: When we do not get the acceptance and confirmation we need in relationships, we are left with a feeling of not being seen or recognized for who we really are. Or, we may fear that others will only respect and love us if we are who *they* want us to be. We may work continuously to feel seen and recognized by others, or we may give up in rage, humiliation, or shame.

6.  **The Fear of Failure and Success**: When we have loved and lost or tried and failed, we may fear the painful competitive experience again. When we have succeeded or won—possibly at someone else's expense—we may experience guilt or fear retaliation. Thus, we learn to hold back in love and life, thereby not risking either failure or success. We may feel the world does not allow us to be fulfilled. Or we may feel guilty and afraid for feeling fulfilled.

7.  **The Fear of Being Full Alive:** Our expansiveness,

creative energy, and joy in our aliveness inevitably come into conflict with family, work, religion, and society. We come to believe that we must curtail our aliveness to conform to the expectations and demands of the world. We feel the world does not permit us to be fully, joyfully, and passionately alive. Rather than putting our whole selves out there with full energy, we may throw in the towel, succumb to mediocre conformity, or fall into living deadness.

## Bringing it All Together

What remains in studying our cumulative primary traumas is for us to take the next step on our own:

1. You can increase your daily mindfulness of your BMR connections by putting on your "Aliveness Monitor" each morning, and "Touching Base with Your Body" whenever you are feeling tense during the day.

2. You can add to your body experiences through yoga, massage, or any other kind of body-focus activities or therapy that feel good to you.

3. You can add to your mental awareness and sensitivity to your experiences through meditation, counseling, or some kind of individual or group psychotherapy or self-focus activity.

The *Overcoming Relationship Fears* book and its accompanying *Workbook* serve as practical guides for overcoming cumulative relational traumas.

*Part Three*
# Re-Experiencing Cumulative Trauma in Relational Psychotherapy: Brief Illustrations

In eighteen published books I have collaborated with more than four hundred therapists over forty years at the Listening Perspectives Study Center and the Newport Psychoanalytic Institute to arrive at the conclusions regarding trauma put forth in this book. Each publication provides in-depth case studies, all of which illustrate in one way or another the effects of cumulative developmental trauma and the re-living of various aspects of that trauma in the transference, resistance, and

What follow are a series of very brief episodes taken from these many case studies that illustrate moments of traumatic re-living in the therapeutic relationship and that point to which of the seven fear countertransference perspectives have been most useful in understanding the underlying primary developmental traumas. Following each case illustration I have provided a footnote for therapists referring to which developmental Listening Perspectives [see Appendix B] I and the therapist have found most helpful in considering this work.

# "I Was Trained to be a Monster"—Blaine

Blaine was the oldest of three siblings with two psychotic parents. In therapy he came to realize his mother was in no way equipped to have children and related to them as though they were the bane of her existence. Early on he learned to create problems for her so she could feel righteous in blaming him for her ineptitudes. She trained him in this way to be monstrous to her and later to his younger siblings—thus creating a constant source of distress for her. Father was emotionally detached but colluded with his wife so that all three children suffered from severe early developmental trauma and life-long cascades of various kinds of secondary relational traumas.

My early attempts to reassure Blaine that I did not abhor him were fruitless. Later when I was able to discuss with him the ways he was off-putting to me as well as to others, he reveled in the confirmation that I truly did hate him and found him to be a monster in the same ways his parents and siblings did. It was the same with friends, work colleagues and siblings. If I and we "weren't exasperated with him" then we were missing the point—that he was *compelled* to exasperate me and everyone else "in order to be loyal to my parents." Repeated rages and tears over months and years occurred over anything and everything that transpired between us. Inadvertently, I was constantly thwarting him and then feeling ashamed of myself—much in the way he felt ashamed of being such a monster to his parents, siblings, and later his friends and work colleagues.

But what gradually became clear was that his "ineptitude and monstrousness" masked his terror of any kind or degree of emotional engagement because his primary relationships of childhood had been so relationally traumatic. That is, he longed for respect and connection but in fact was terrified of any relating that moved toward emotional involvement since all attempts at mutual affect regulation in infancy and toddlerhood had ended in gut wrenching painful aloneness—"like I am flying helplessly through the blackness of outer space, for all purposes dead to the world, unable to meaningfully connect to anyone."

The first two fears—the fear of being alone and the fear of connecting proved most useful in understanding the many enactments we mutually engaged in over the years. That is, at moments either I would move emotionally toward him or respond to his emotional overtures toward me and he would "quickly cut off the reaching tendrils." Therapeutic progress was slow so that after a long period of us learning to trust each other we could mark those moments of potential contact and then work together to hold ourselves together with each other for brief moments that, over time, could be extended and then generalized into other relationships in his life. [15]

## "I Want You Dead So I Can Be Myself"—Carley

Carley experienced an emotional breakdown in her first semester at college that was some miles from home. For months she was hospitalized with a series of psychotic diagnoses with bipolar as well as obsessive-compulsive features and an eating disorder. She was under the care of a psychiatrist and heavily medicated. Her parents insisted that she come to therapy to get her life together. A careful history conducted with both parents by a colleague revealed very intelligent good-enough parents who had raised three other very well-adjusted children. It was reported by mother that "she came out of the womb screaming and from the beginning demanded incessantly to be fed until she would spit up." With hindsight the possibility exists that there had been gestational diabetes or some other constitutional nutritional anomaly though at the time nothing had been tested for—but gestational diabetes was diagnosed with a younger sibling and treated accordingly.

From the beginning Carley hated and mistrusted me believing that therapy was for the purpose of forcing her to be and do as her parents, society, friends and the entire mental health system wanted her to. Slowly profound trust evolved so that she came to believe that I was the only person in her life who had ever understood and respected her. She would often race to thrice-weekly sessions early because she had so much to go over with me. In keeping with her generation she also sent frequent texts and emails—especially when I would be traveling and teaching, even when I was halfway around the world.

Carley's recurring split between severe distrust and hatred versus trust, respect, and love vacillated frequently. What emerged was a lifetime of experienced social attractions and rebuffs that sent her either into depressed isolation or manic episodes that served to deny the lack of emotional connectedness. Whatever apparently had happened before birth had left Carley ill prepared to set up mutually rewarding emotional resonance with her mother, family members, teachers, or friends. That she was extremely intelligent and overall physically attractive and good natured brought people to her. But her disillusioned rages because they expected "unrealistic and demeaning mutual emotional interactions" with her sent them running. The central repeated cry was, "I want to be my own person, free to live as I want, not always having to do things the way you, my parents, my friends, society and all of the idiots in the mental health field want me to.

Primary pre-birth trauma experiences set Carley up for a cascade of repeated traumatic experiences when she was unable to obtain the kind of understanding, nurturing, mirroring responses from others that she craved. She and I both suffered in the transference and countertransference involvements as we would come together for periods in hope and good will only to have our sustaining connection suddenly thwarted and spit up. Using the visual metaphor of a mother and baby joyously and mutually interacting until "something happened" to blow the connection and collapse the baby, Carley chose the word "competency" to characterize what she could not tolerate. That is, whether with myself, with peers, with family, with academics, or with creative endeavors just when she would get going strong and begin to feel competent some invisible internalized something would happen to interrupt, to rupture, to destroy the connection—presumably a recapitulation of early emotional connecting experience. Watching over time the repeated disruptions of her competency—often with psychotic symptoms like severe obsessive-compulsive behaviors, eating fads or manic/depressive flights, Carley became aware of underlying terrors in every endeavor, in every relationship—especially ours. Amassing courage and determination she began moment by moment, episode by episode, to anticipate fear and avoidance of competent connections and to take steps to plant her feet and emotions firmly and push ahead no matter how potentially shattering her successes were. Of course, I fell repeatedly into enacting upsetting moments with her and then having to shame-faced apologize for my insensitivities. Throughout

71

all of this I had to "play the grandfather card"—that is, work hard not to be frightening, especially since her eating disorder was laced with eroticism that I often stepped carefully around—though we could talk of her various desires to seduce me and others into merging into eternal (eroticized) bliss with her. As she learned not only to tolerate but to revel in her successes I enacted a proud parent/supportive coach role until she could begin to internalized these functions. It wasn't that her parents weren't warm and supportive but the traumatic failures of presumably pre-birth experience had to be titrated with a person who could tolerate the constant, angry, devaluing, ungrateful disconnects—something really hard for even the most devoted parents to accomplish.

The second fear of being terrified to connect because early emotional connections had felt hurtful and anger-provoking was our most useful perspective. But when depressive and manic themes prevailed they seemed to both be defensive reactions to the first fear of being desperately and terrifyingly alone in the universe. Suffice it to say that we were constantly on the edge of paranoia, worried that I or others were thinking bad things about her, hating her, or wanting to take advantage or seduce her. The therapeutic process involved a long period of mutual trust building followed by working on feelings of terrifying loneliness, emptiness, and worthlessness. At last she began the painstaking work on connections with others and with her own body/self in order to tolerate the terror of reaching out and achieving personal and interpersonal competence. We slowly got past the mutual disconnecting enactments and began to achieve mutual affect regulation that characterizes human symbiosis. Carley has confidence that we will grow together from here—already taking pride in her accomplishments (perspective three) is setting in![16]

Audubon

# Atlantic Puffin

After suffering major declines in the 19th and 20th centuries, Atlantic Puffins are rebounding today — thanks to an ambitious Audubon effort to re-introduce the seabirds on their former nesting islands off the coast of Maine. But as climate change and warming waters threaten puffins' continued success, they are counting on concerned bird lovers like you to help them cope, adapt, and thrive.

Please visit **audubon.org/bird-guide** to learn more about this adorable, captivating species and other iconic birds across North America.

Atlantic Puffins.
Photo: Jean Hall/Audubon Photography Awards

Audubon

National Audubon Society
225 Varick Street, 7th Floor
New York, NY 10014
www.audubon.org

Q2110INB

# "With Everyone I am Compelled to 'Service Mother'"—Christopher

Christopher was born into rural poverty with a schizophrenic mother and an autistic father but was endowed with native intelligence enough to learn even as an infant that he could ferret out or even create moments of emotional involvement with his mother that he needed for development—unlike his siblings who could not do so and were resultingly abysmally and pathologically undeveloped. He early on learned to do what he later came to call "serving her in everything I do, with everyone I meet." Needless to say, in later life he developed a penchant for women that needed to be emotionally salvaged and served. After several marriages and a series of disastrous relationships with women he called "borderline", he sought therapy because he was sure even if an emotionally whole and mature woman stood directly in front of him he could not see her since his world was completely populated with false-self women who needed a trophy man to fill in gaps in their self-esteem.

Over time as this "service mode" gradually transferred into our relationship he became certain that he was to service my poor self-esteem needs and became repeatedly enraged at the ways he found that I was using him and abusing him for my own purposes. At some level he felt his mother had molested him and he was sure I wanted to do the same. Since he was a very bright man he was always able to discern something in my demeanor, behavior, emotional resonance, or speech that filled the bill for defining his experiences. We spent many sessions agonizing together over his fate to ferret out aspects of myself that he had to service—or at least believed he had to—and details that seemed to prove uncompromisingly my wish to exploit him.

It was much to my chagrin when at times I found myself mutually enacting his service mode with him. At last he was able to rage and sob repeatedly every time another repetition of his perception appeared and became enacted. He needed me to cop to whatever pieces were genuine mistakes or misunderstandings on my part, or even inadvertent or unconscious slips so that he could be clear how his inner world of infant and life-long cascading traumas had been triggered by whatever had realistically happened between us. Predominant in our early work together was the horrifying fear of abandonment if either he or I failed to service adequately. Then slowly emerged the fear of emotionally connecting either positively or negatively. He began to realize that virtually nowhere in his life was he safe to connect. This led to a deep "suicidal" regression in the sense that he encountered his fear that he was helplessly and hopelessly alone in the world with no reason to be alive. His horrible mental and physical pains of despair came to be understood as "memories" of his earliest experiences with an unavailable mother with whom he subsequently figured out how to entice by rescuing and servicing her needs. Inch by painful inch Christopher began in every relationship and aspect of his life to abstain from servicing and to look for mutually engaging connections — of which he was afraid and distrustful.[17]

## "I Had to Die for Mother"—Darrin, Part One

Darrin was in advanced stages of his therapy when he finally acknowledged that he had been forever addicted to prescription pills for sleeping. From time to time he had made attempts (with and without help of various kinds) to relinquish his habit of nightly sleeping pills. During the six-week period of letting go of his addiction he made frequent contact with me by phone and scheduling extra sessions. Darrin even had to take time off work several days during this period because of extreme fatigue and intense painful agony in all parts of his body due to his withdrawal from the medication.

Darrin was determined to discover the inner relationship scenario that compelled him to resort to prescription drugs. For several weeks he allowed himself the luxury of wandering around the house in his pajamas. He added the humorous touch of carrying a teddy bear. He soon found himself able to catch "cat naps" under the dining room table with his teddy and "blankie"—though he was aware during these naps of being hyper-alert to sounds and movements in the house. Darrin even put warm milk in a bottle to see if that would bring out more early memories! Without the pills he couldn't sleep a wink at night. So for awhile he dragged around desperately tired and miserable during the day.

Darrin studied all of his physical and emotional reactions to being without his pills. He soon developed the odd conviction that I wanted him to be miserable and to moan and drag around in desperate agony! "I feel like I'm supposed to die for you," he wailed—not quite realizing at the time what he was saying.

At this point Darrin made the decision to tell his mother about his life-long plight in hopes she could help him recover memories of what traumas he must have experienced in his early life. Several interesting stories emerged. Mother had desperately wanted a baby. She clung to Darrin from the moment he was born. Her physical and emotional needs for a cuddly baby quickly taught Darrin an intolerance of physical separation from her. When Father later forced him out of the parental bed and yet later out of the parental bedroom, Darrin cried bitterly and intractably at night. Father, with rage and occasional physical violence, forbade Mother to rescue Darrin in the nightly scenes. Darrin would cry, kick, scream, and finally convulse in his crib—relentless in his demand for Mother. The doctor supported Father in his belief that the boy should be allowed to "cry it out" until they "broke him." But every night, after seemingly interminable angry, desperate, agonizing protests from Darrin—just when the child was about to die from choking and exhaustion, Mother would defy Father and creep into Darrin's room. She found it necessary to spend the remainder of the night in the rocking chair by the crib holding the baby so he could sleep. Darrin thus learned to stay awake and to be miserable until at last she came. That is, he learned to be miserable, to "almost die" for her. But the story and the family web which remembers or commemorates intergenerational mothering subsequently becomes even more entangled.

In talking with his parents Darrin fully realized what bad shape their marriage had always been in. A year before, he had urged his mother into therapy for listlessness, depression, and feelings of meaninglessness and uselessness. It seems Darrin's mother, thirty-five years later, was still sitting in the same rocker. She pleaded with her son to return to their home town and set up his business near her which he knew was a bad idea.

In her therapy Mother worked on the trauma of her life which she could now, for the first time, share with Darrin. When she was around two years of age she and her slightly older brother accompanied their mother to the chicken coop in an isolated rural area to gather eggs during a break in one of those frightening Midwest thunderstorms with fierce wind, dark clouds, and terrifying lightening The children were clinging to Mother's skirt when she slipped in the mud, spilling the eggs and injuring herself. Father asked neighbors to rush him and his wife to the hospital fifty miles away. Father left the children in the care of his own mother for three weeks. He returned grief stricken—without Mother. No attempt was made to explain their mother's untimely death to the children or to include them in the funeral plans. Darrin's mother related with sobs and shaking how for years she had sat in her little rocking chair by the window waiting desperately for her mother to return. "Where is Mother? Why did she go away? Doesn't she love me? Doesn't she need me? When will she come back?"

Darrin's mother married a man as emotionally absent as her father. But when Darrin was born, the emotional void left by the abrupt and mysterious abandonment of her mother was at last filled. Her husband and the doctor colluded in replicating her internal childhood scenario by cruelly forbidding her the connection with her beloved baby which she so desperately needed in order to feel once again enlivened.

In therapy Darrin soon realized that his inability to go to sleep without pills was for her—a living memorial to his mother's desperate and dependent love for him. The pill addiction substituted for her warm body and allowed him to sleep. The instructions built into his internal scenario were that he was not to drift off to sleep without her. So he could only risk hyper-vigilant cat naps that were not in his bed where he might accidentally fall asleep. Darrin also discovered the strange fear that if he went to sleep he would surely die—a role reversal of a scenario that was an accurate reading of his mother's unconscious fear of losing her mother. Darrin's loud protests of need for his mother throughout the night allowed Mother in her internal scenario to at last feel needed and wanted. In his near-death desperation as a child Darrin replaced her own lost mother—but now she could override her childhood helplessness trauma and this time be the rescuer.

With these mind-body connections having been made through therapy, Darrin took his blankie and teddy to bed and slept for three solid days and nights! His need to stay up for her at any cost and his pill addiction (to substitute for Mother's finally coming and allowing him to sleep) were at last ended. The unconscious relationship pattern of the scenario was broken. Likewise, his fears that either he or his mother would die if he gave up his vigil—the emotional role reversal of the internal scenario—the parent part, was over. The fear perspective most helpful in this portion of his analysis was the fear of being abandoned with an intergenerational twist. In therapy Darrin was constantly worried that I would disappear or be too preoccupied with other things to respond to his needs. In fact, at times he created crises that I needed to respond to. There were frequently episodes in Darrin's life at this point that were full of realistic dangers and I found myself often worried for his sake and urging him to be careful and take care of himself, I didn't want anything to happen to him—mutual enactments to be sure. [18]

## "I Saw Barbara with Straw Hat and Feather Boa"—Darrin Continued

Darrin's therapy opened with his parading extravagant and

fashionable clothes, shoes, and stylish haircuts for me. Even his workout clothes and shoes were elegant. Shortly after he told his mother he was in therapy she prepared a life scrapbook with the most incredible set of childhood mother and son pictures I have ever seen — to show to his therapist. The child had been adorably costumed since infancy and placed in extraordinary settings with outlandish props that highlighted not only his very handsome looks but his camera savvy and his confident, winning smile. Whenever I asked where his mother was when this shot was taken he knew because he always posed for her. Only a few photos tangentially showed father or his two years older brother. Darrin identified as gay and exerted incredible power in drawing men rapidly into his bed. He spoke openly about his seductive behavior toward me but at no time was he realistically concerned that either of us would lose our boundaries. Darrin at times hoped he could learn to have sex with a woman and made several failed attempts — concluding that women were somehow forbidden but he wasn't sure just why. What was exciting to him was the kind of awe, envy, and admiration he could draw from a seducing a man.

As the history unfolded it seems that the first son was "Daddy's boy" and taken completely away from mother. She hoped her next child would be a girl so she could have the kind of symbiotic oneness she had always longed for since her symbiosis with her mother had been so cruelly interrupted. Said Darrin, "she made me into the girl she always wanted, all of those scrapbook pictures make that clear." One day he arrived at therapy triumphant, "I know who she is — Barbara in an outrageous yellow dress with a big straw hat, sunglasses, and a feather boa, all perched on the back of a parading white Cadillac convertible smiling and waving ecstatically at the adoring crowds. Thereafter his peacock presentation abruptly relaxed as he realized that all of this demand to be seen, admired, adored was a trauma he had endured for her and transferred to men since she didn't want to lose him to a woman. This portion of his analysis was best understood with his fear of being seen, appreciated and respected for who he is. No longer afraid to truly strut his competences in the world, the defensive elegant, slightly swishy parade demeanor (for mother and me) could be relinquished as he and I could see both his worldly effectiveness and his essential manliness.[19]

## "The Doctor Is Interfering with My Birth"— Gregory

Brief episodes are unconvincing of anything because they only exist at a moment in time and necessarily omit the vast emotional underpinnings of the relational work that preceded them. I was recently at a conference in which a medical therapist presented a clinical hour attempting to illustrate the operation of Bion's "O"— that is, the operation of the unknown and unknowable in therapeutic transformations. Most of the reported clinical hour with Gregory appeared relatively commonplace in the client's narration of current life events with family, friends, and wife as well as discussion of the forthcoming birth of his first child. At some point during the hour the therapist reports to the audience that as the session proceeded he was experiencing a growing tension in his arms and chest during the session that caught his attention. In his reverie he likened the tension to the times when he, with extended arms and chest had delivered babies in medical training. With only a few minutes left to the hour the client suddenly remembers a dream from the previous night. He is in an institutional setting watching a baby being delivered. But the doctor is trying to force the baby back into the womb. The client leaps forward in horror and rage yelling, "That's all wrong, that's not the way to do it!" Associating to the dream the client is perplexed about what it meant until the analyst quietly suggests, "perhaps it has something to do with what's going on with us." There is a sinking thud as the client's head drops into his hands and a deep sigh as the client emotionally grasps the depth of the transference/countertransference enactments that the dream portrays as the session comes to a close.

One questioner wanted to know how this was any different from any transference interpretation. The presenter merely nodded. Another therapist commented on the everyday quality of the therapist's countertransference experiencing—that is, a fairly simple projective identification. The presenter merely nodded again. Finally, someone spoke to what most of us could understand as the total mystery of therapeutic moments of deep reverie and emotional attunement like this that permit the client to drop into deep relational anguish that allows an instantaneous emotional recapitulation of a cascade of childhood traumatic moments transferred into the therapeutic relationship. The interpersonal fears of failing and/or succeeding in the competitive triangular relationships involving his wife and n e w b o r n son as well as his triangular relationships with them and his therapist emerge in this dream as an independent triangulating part of him insists on being born.[20]

# Aurora Struggles in her Triangular Relationships

Since antiquity the potentially tragic effects of triangular emotional relationships have been well-known. The great myths and dramas of all time portray a hero or heroine caught up in some sort of a competitive love triangle. Oedipus in his love for his mother was caught up in competitive feelings with his father. Electra in her love for her father was caught up in competitive feelings with her mother.

Aurora's parents separated when she was three but she experienced in her upbringing a respectful and cooperative atmosphere between them. In her mid-twenties she married Serge whom she admired for the way he cared for her and his stated ambitions in life. As the relationship developed, however, Serge became unbearably possessive and controlling, experiencing intense jealousy over her relationships with her family and her lifelong friends as well as her newly formed school and business friends. His stated ambitions deteriorated into a general passivity. Most of the time he sat in front of the television watching sports.

As Aurora struggled to define her position in individual and couples counseling, she encountered deep-seated rage at her mother who, while always seeming to promise a special relationship with Aurora, in fact often emotionally deferred to her new husband in a way that left Aurora feeling emotionally left out. Aurora was able to turn to her father for understanding and support while working on resolving her angry feelings at her sense of emotional abandonment by her mother.

Later in counseling Aurora got in touch with her rage at her father for his preoccupations with his work and his own love relationships which she had always experienced as emotionally excluding her. At this point she was able to turn toward her mother for support in working out her rageful feelings toward her father.

Growing up as an only child with parents who were divorced at an early age had made it difficult for Aurora to experience and work through emotional triangles as a young child. As a result she was having to work through triangular relationship experiences in the context of having a husband who was unable to tolerate the competition of her loving relationships with her family and friends. Her distress in her marriage brought up her triangular relationship fear reflexes from childhood.

In the process of getting in touch with her fear reflexes regarding succeeding and failing in emotional triangles, Aurora realized that she could not stay in a marriage ruled by controlling jealousy. In the turmoil of the separation and divorce she experienced considerable anxiety and a variety of stress symptoms that affected various parts of her body.

Aurora met Nicole in the cafeteria at the company where she worked. Nicole's husband had died several years earlier from pancreatic cancer as a young man. Both women were looking for a bonded relationship in which they could safely love and be loved. They longed for a relationship in which they could each experience strong loving relationships with friends and family as well. They soon moved in together and established a deeply committed relationship based on mutual love and respect. In time, they arranged a beautiful marriage ceremony with family and friends. Only later after court rulings was it possible to legalize the marriage.

It was only a matter of time before Aurora and Nicole found

themselves wanting to share their love with a child. Who would carry the baby? Where would the sperm come from? Would their child know and have a relationship with the biological father? Would they be able to provide needed father figures for the child to relate to? How would friends and family react? Given the support each of them had experienced from their own parents in the course of growing up, how would they each as parents be able to establish a loving relationship with a child within a cooperative and inevitably competitive love triangle? Only time would tell. Throughout these episodes we see Aurora struggling with competing and cooperating triangular relationship with the ongoing fears of success and failure cropping up at every turn.[21]

## So Much to Do, So Little Time—Marcie

To say Marcie has too many things on her plate would be an understatement. She is a high-energy woman with a smile and a word of encouragement for everyone. When it's time to get something done, call Marcie. She'll spend half the night if necessary getting the award banquet table decorations ready. She never hesitates to do more than her share of driving in the kids' car pool and for after-school and weekend activities. If phone calls have to be made to remind people of a meeting or e-mails need to be sent out—you can count on Marcie. When a new president of the board is needed, there is Marcie—competent, ready, and available. When there are squabbles to be settled Marcie's the one who can handle things tactfully and effectively. "The trouble with me is I can't say no."

Marcie certainly doesn't *look* lifeless. But she pays a heavy price for giving her all to each group adventure she is a part of, for not guarding her personal boundaries more carefully from social intrusions, for not valuing her personal, individualized inner life more than group expectations, and for not treasuring her intimate relationships more dearly.

In my years of being Marcie's therapist I can only remember once her telling of a day she fixed herself a tuna sandwich and took a great book into her back yard and had a perfectly delicious afternoon by herself reading, enjoying the spring breezes and gentle sunshine in her garden.

Marcie grew up in a large family in a northwest farming community. From as early as she can remember everyone relied on her to get things moving, to make things happen, to organize the chores, to cheer everyone up. Exactly when her father's alcoholism began to insert itself insidiously into family life isn't quite clear. But it was Marcie's job to manage him, to protect the others from his abuses, to see that he got to bed safely. Where was mother all this time? Needless to say, Marcie was always the class president, the athletic team captain, the year book editor. In high school and college she graduated with high honors. She met Nathan, her husband, at a college weekend get-together, but since they were each committed to different graduate school programs in nearby states their early years together were spent weekend commuting.

Children came along, but because Nathan's job required him be on the road much of the time, the week-end marital intimacy and family life has continued indefinitely.

Every circumstance in Marcie's life requires her to wear another hat—and she wears them all well. She has learned how to fit in well at church, at the kids' schools, in her profession, in the neighborhood, in the community, in her husband's company group and among their set of close friends. Whatever the demand Marcie finds some way to rise to the occasion. Most of the time Marcie feels energetic and well—though she spends a lot of time at her shrink's and her chiropractor's offices. Otherwise everything with Marcie is great!

What's wrong with this picture? Marcie simply isn't fully alive to herself. Living for her own pleasure and satisfaction with her own desires, hopes and goals is somehow forbidden by her fear of being fully alive reflexes. She has no right to a fulfilling life of her own. Marcie's cascade of traumas is difficult to specify since she did, after all attain a quite mature development and is high functioning in the world. Only when she discovered Nathan had a mistress did she begin to look seriously at her high functioning and realize that she had deprived herself of the pleasures of emotional intimacy her entire life. The dominant fear perspective Marcie and I found helpful was the seventh fear, her fear of not being everything to everybody. Yes, at times we reverted to triangular fears of her husband and her children or his friends. At other times the fears of abandonment predominated and perhaps most deeply the fear of being alone in the universe that kept her manically and frantically creating all kinds of relationships.[22]

# Dream: "The Invasion of the Chili Pepper Monsters"—Larry

The last illustration is a somewhat humorous portrayal of the effects of cumulative invasive stimulation. Over twenty years ago when I was working on completing an early draft of *Overcoming Relational Fears* I was reading through the seventh deadly fear, the fear of being fully alive, which I had formulated as a composite of all of the relational fears we have accumulated over a lifetime in which culture and society itself serves as "the third" which inhibits being fully and passionately alive. As I was drifting off to sleep I was trying to imagine what the experience of feeling afraid to be fully alive felt like at the body level. I awoke in a cold sweat with fear and trembling from the following nightmarish dream.

I was at home with someone who seemed like another part of myself, like an alter ego. There were other shadowy figures in the background like the ghosts of my family and friends. I was vaguely afraid and alert to some impending danger. Suddenly I saw what looked like long tentacles creeping through the crack under my door. They were long—maybe three or four feet—and there was a sense of many more tentacled creatures pushing to get in. Some were trying to poke their way in through a crevice in the ceiling. Others-wiggled in through the air vents. I couldn't actually see the monsters trying to force their way in. Only their reaching, probing, invading tentacles were visible. But I had a sense that they came in all sizes up to 5 or 6 feet long.

I knew somehow that these tentacles belonged to 'chili pepper monsters'—they were long, thin, pointed, dark red, and somewhat flat and pliable. Only the long pointed end actually entered my space. The top part (the other two points of the triangular form of the tentacles) remained outside under control of the monsters. I knew that these chili pepper monsters killed people—not by violence, but by taking them in—by forcing others to become like them, to become one of them! I was surrounded by these chili pepper monsters with tentacles reaching in through every possible crack and crevice.

I somehow managed to shoo them out temporarily—to keep them at bay for awhile. But I was becoming increasingly frantic, feeling I was losing the battle, that they were coming in from everywhere, that I was surrounded and vastly outnumbered, that there was nothing I could do to stop them. I called to the other who was with me, 'get the insecticide!' It turned out to be a whitish-yellow powder (the color of whitewash) that I could sprinkle on the tentacles. The repressing powder caused the tentacles to withdraw and to disappear temporarily from view, though it didn't actually kill or get rid of them—it only kept them at temporarily bay.

I called out to the other with me, 'where was it we were going? We have to clear a path out of here! We have to hurry!' The line sounded like an ironic, hopeless-comic line from Samuel Becket's *Waiting for Godot*. The comic element came in the vague realization that I was planning an escape from the clearly inescapable. We were surrounded, outnumbered, and ultimately in danger of being overpowered by them—we didn't have a chance. There was no way out and I knew it! I thought, 'how silly of me to think I can escape them, they're everywhere—creeping, crawling, wriggling tentacles trying to pry their way into my space, trying to take me over and make me into one of themselves!'

I braced myself in terror when I realized there was no escape. I awoke with a start—sweating from tossing and turning. I was curled up in a tight fetal position. My body was shaking, totally tense and constricted, and my heart was racing.

I thought immediately that these 'chili pepper monsters,' were mildly addictive (seductive) and edible (oedipal) in nature! The shape of the red tentacles with their threatening points intruding was basically triangular. The other two points were outside of my abode and under control of monstrous intruders that were threatening my personal existence from all directions. Triangular tentacles were everywhere threatening to take me over—there was no escape!

I thought of the 'shrinking the fear monster' exercise I had read in *Overcoming Relational Fears* the night before. I had fallen asleep wondering what the Fear of Being Fully Alive might actually look like in my body. In my dream I visualized my Fear of Being Fully Alive as a horde of triangle shaped, intrusive tentacles belonging to the addictive chili pepper monsters. My dream pictured my inner world threatened by an endless and inescapable invasion of outside (social) threats.

I had read the night before in *Overcoming Relational Fears* that all relationships are influenced by external social forces of a triangular nature that are not completely under our own control. The extent to which we surrender ourselves to others in love is the extent to which our individual selves, our own needs and desires, our carefully carved out self-integrity feels the danger of an invasive threat.

As a child I was continuously invaded by intense needs and demands of my parents to be certain ways and not to be other ways. I learned my own secret ways of holing up in the safe seclusion of my private self development with my own inner dialogue (the alter-ego in the dream). I had to isolate myself emotionally from my family in order to protect myself from succumbing to the powerful (and to a child, monstrous) forces that I felt surrounded me. I have always tried to repress, to whitewash, the extent of my fear of the invasive influence of others on myself."

In our journey toward greater aliveness things come at us every day that are frightening, that we brace ourselves against. But we have for so long conditioned ourselves not to actually experience fear that we fail to notice how profoundly we are affected by powerful and intrusive social forces. Cultivating full aliveness implies developing a heightened sensitivity to all of the intrusive and disturbing group influences that impinge on us in the course of a day.

We do not give our best to others when we pull back short of what we could give—short of where we could reach if we made the effort. We tend to stop short of what we could be—dominated by a plague of irrational and unconscious monstrous fears masquerading as anxiety, tension, fatigue, stress, anger, illness, and depression. How many of us can honestly name a single relationship in which we have been willing and able to give our all to its fulfillment, no matter how frightened we were of the intimacy and commitment involved? We are painfully aware of how we shortchange the ones we love—our partners, our friends, our children, our parents, and our work colleagues. Now we can become aware of how our fear of Being Fully Alive shortchanges us!

# Part Four

# Interpersonal/Relational Psychotherapy: Lengthy Illustrations

## *'Night, Mother*—Sarah Turner-Miller[23]

Bioenergetic therapist Dr. Sarah Turner-Miller recounts a year-long saga with her client, Maggie, whom she describes as a middle-aged woman, groomed but untidy with a worn, thrift-store look. Her large eyes not only stare but seem to look completely through Sarah. Clutching her purse she declares that therapy is her last stop. She tells Sarah that she is agitated and cannot sleep; that she feels ugly like she does not belong on earth, like she doesn't exist.

Maggie was adopted at 4 months of age. Her adoptive parents had two older sons. Maggie bonded with her father, who died when she was 10. Mother remarried and her new husband had a son who had sex in the afternoon with different people and masturbated in front of her. She received no protection. "My mother is like a black apple. I feel pain and darkness—no hope. Why bother? I'm tired. Nothing works."

Sarah struggles to establish a connection with Maggie. Every now and then she sees a flash in Maggie's eyes that acknowledges that she is there. Sarah feels morbid when she is with Maggie, craving rest and sun. She feels she is with a person who is already dead as if Sarah has to provide meaningful existence for both of them. Maggie clearly craves some kind of sustained connection, some symbiotic tie with Sarah even though paradoxically it seems somehow life-threatening to her. Maggie unconsciously knows her limited experience of symbiosis to be so destructive that she loses either way—with or without connection. She wants Sarah to be a successful mother to her and to pull her from her deep schizoid withdrawal.

Sarah experiences Maggie as filling the room with a hostile oozing energy that is full of vile hatred. Sarah finds herself thinking: "I hate you! I hate you! Go away—disappear—don't kill yourself; just get out of my space. The countertransference is so pervasive and persistent that Sarah can hardly breathe, but now she knows how hated Maggie was. Says Sarah: "She needs to know I know, to feel that I have some sense of how hated she was. She needs to hear that I mourn her lost humanity and that I cringe at her deadening processes."

The countertransference needs to somehow be spoken. Sarah hesitatingly begins,

> I have some very important things to share with you today. These are feelings, thoughts, observations about myself when I'm with you that may help us understand your difficulties even more….What happened to you was so early in your life there is no way for you to tell me just how terrible you feel. There is only the therapeutic dance that goes on between us for you to show me what goes on deep inside of you….As we get to know one another I essentially become, in psychic experience, you the infant and you become your parents. Thus I come to know your experience by living out your inner life. …Often and from the very beginning, I have experienced intense feelings that do not seem to be mine. I feel scared and confused around you. I feel I am not enough for you—that there is

some awesome rage and chaos that I can't get out of easily. I feel depleted, drained of my life. I feel evil. ...When I try to connect with you, I feel destroyed in my efforts. We know this is not your intention; not you, consciously. You are showing me something important. (pp 130-131)

Maggie seemed somewhat dazed by this session and I checked on her later by phone. The next session Maggie brought in two watercolor paintings that she said were provoked by our last meeting. One was a pregnant woman painted black with a fetus of blue with a red center. The other was a design with a dark center. She said, "This is what it's like to be in the black hole. It starts at the center and bleeds out, the black hole contains it, controls it, and won't let it live....I know you know something about us and I feel calmer."

Next Maggie brought Sarah her "bad stuff" in a brown paper bag. Bad stuff refers to her favorite morbid movies, but she explains that she has left the most important one at home. Shortly Maggie phones Sarah to tell her that she wants to kill herself and believes she can. Sarah convinces her to go to her trusted gynecologist and he got her to a psychiatrist who prescribed Prozac and Xanax.

Maggie then brings her favorite video, 'Night, Mother, for safekeeping in Sarah's office. 'Night, Mother is a play by Marsha Norman that probes deeply into a mother-daughter symbiosis that ends in a suicide dance of the deepest despair and loneliness.

Maggie happens upon the movie which becomes her transitional object. She has watched it hundreds of times. The interaction between daughter Jessie and her Mama has struck a deep place within Maggie. She, like Jessie, wishes to die and knows that her life as she lives it has to end. She is morbidly invested in every word. She wants Sarah to join in.

The movie portrays the evening in which Jessie tells her mother she is going to kill herself that night. We follow the two through gripping conversations in which painful aspects of Jessie's life, including her struggle with epilepsy, are worked over by the two. Jessie hurriedly rushes down the hall with Mama following screaming and banging on the locked door until the fatal gunshot is heard. "Jessie, Jessie, child ... Forgive me. (Pause) I thought you were mine."

Maggie wants Sarah to play 'Night, Mother with her. Watching the movie and reading the script has enlightened Sarah about the nature of the transference-countertransference matrix she has felt so desperately caught up into.

> I feel like I've been struck in the head by lightning bolts. She carries the video around in a paper bag. She leaves it in my office for safekeeping with a great deal of pomp and circumstance. She tells me that as long as I have 'Night, Mother in my possession, she won't do anything to hurt herself. She promises to leave it with me for so many weeks, then asks for it in the next session. Keep this dangerous movie away from me, she begs and then sneers at me and insists on having it back that instant! In spite of the rich material we discuss at length, the obsession exhausts us both. (p.136)

Finally Sarah has had enough:

> I've had it with this 'Night, Mother spook show. I hate feeling responsible for keeping Maggie alive, as if I could. I know the agony of Mama. It's my turn to let her know

94

how much I detest being in this position. The dialogue from that session went like this: "I can't be warm and caring when you turn me into a hospital or police person whose job is to keep you from killing yourself. I don't want that job! Your most important way to relate to life is in the 'Night, Mother game. I cannot play it with you. I will not be your "'Night, Mother." It's not right for me. You've got to stop this! When you endanger your life, you can't have me....Jessie had the last word with Mama, the blast of a gun. I know you're looking for a way to have the last word with me....I really want to relate to you. We can connect in a real way; as two warm loving humans. (p. 136)

Maggie says somehow our last session when "You blew up at me" helped her to get some things into a new perspective, that she could feel Sarah better. She watched 'Night, Mother again....This time she saw a girl who had lived a lifetime of pain that she never expressed to anyone and how no one picked up on her pain, so they thought everything was fine. She also saw someone who was already dead basically; that killing herself was just the completion of the physical act of something that had long been dead.

She tells Sarah that she now knows that Sarah understands. That Jesse is someone who had been hurt all her life, yet had not given voice to that pain until that one evening when it all came out. Maggie told Sarah that she now understands why she identifies so much with that movie. She's going to read the script again to see if she can experience it from a different perspective.

Maggie shortly reports feeling more balanced. She even smiles at Sarah now.

Maggie says she almost trusts Sarah, that she can see the craziness of *'Night, Mother* and how she used to feel a victim of it. She dreams, "I asked you what do you think of your daughter? You said, 'I couldn't do without her. She's so good.'"

Soon Maggie wants a clean break from therapy so the two went through several months of termination. Maggie has no money and Sarah has been carrying a bill up to $5,000 because Maggie needed the therapy and because Sarah has feared for her life.

Two months after termination Maggie filed for bankruptcy, her whereabouts unknown.

Sarah:

> It's as if the therapy was her birthright—that she shouldn't have to pay to exist in my office. What she owed me is really what was owed to her in nature a thousand times over: a real mother with goodness and love. Emotional bankruptcy was filed on her a long time ago. She played it out to the bitter end. From the position Maggie left me in I can now say, knowing what it means to her, "Good night, Mother." But at least it is I who am symbolically left for dead and she, as survivor, is on her own to find her way in the world.
>
> Wherever Maggie is, I wish her well. (p. 139)[24]

—

# "I Am Going to Die"—Audrey Seaton-Bacon[25]

You are about to encounter two years of very difficult work begun at a doctoral-level training clinic by Dr. Audrey Seaton-

Bacon who carried her work with Anne Marie into private practice after graduation.

> "Will you sit by me?" "Will you hold my hand?" "Can I lean on you?" "Will you hold me?" "Please don't hurt me!" "Help me!" "I can't find you!" "I'm scared!" "What's happening to me?" "I can't make it!" "I have to hit myself." "I am going to die."

These statements and questions expressed the need and the terror that Anne Marie felt as she and Audrey immersed themselves into the depths of her internalized Organizing experience.

Training to be a therapist rarely prepares students for this type of intense need, this regressed and frightening demand for closeness that is destined to stir up feelings of destruction and self-destruction. In fact, training supervisors are often so preoccupied with teaching "correct technique" and malpractice concerns that clients with such primitive needs are often overlooked or severely neglected. Says Audrey Seaton-Bacon:

> For Anne Marie, the terror came in her reaching out for connection. She had not been emotionally connected with anyone for much, if not most, of her life. She struggled to be emotionally present. Physical contact was the only way she knew how to, and could, stay present. She regressed back into what seemed to be her first month of life. With wide-eyed innocence and intensity, she searched for the other—me. Her reaching out produced fears of being hurt, abandoned, dropped, and dying. Her body betrayed her with memories she could not identify and memories of being sexually abused. She recoiled. She reached. She recoiled

97

and reached until, several months into the process, we made contact. The connection we finally achieved was immensely satisfying to both of us. It was intense with aliveness. All our senses betrayed us. We giggled. We watched each other. We imitated each other. We played. We found each other. We disconnected. (pp 186-7)

When Audrey was asked to write up this case for publication she reports that she found herself spoiling—minimizing, destroying, and ignoring—the request. She feared exposing her own struggles that were going on in the depth of the transference/countertransference entanglement.

Anne Marie had attempted therapy several times before to address her history of childhood sexual abuse, anorexia, and bulimia. After an abortive attempt at marital counseling she was ready for deep individual therapy. In the early months of therapy Anne Marie talked of "feeling shaky inside," her fear of being hurt, and her feelings of being empty.

Anne Marie related intellectually, but not affectively, with others in her life. When she did finally begin to experience emotions, they were ambitendent—i.e., alternating good and bad feelings of equal intensity. She reported feeling that she does not belong anywhere but as the work took shape she began to experience the intensity of her own neediness and quickly grew more dependent on Audrey. Her critical attitude toward her neediness and dependency was interpreted as her internalized parents' response to her neediness, and as an overall attempt to prevent or break any connection she made with Audrey.

As Anne Marie regressed, she demanded more of me. There

were times that she struggled to find me. Sitting across from her seemed too far out of reach. She asked me to sit beside her. She needed me closer, but the closeness triggered memories from her past. She struggled to stay present. She reached her hand out for me to hold in a desperate attempt to stay present. I held on feeling helpless and conflicted. She flinched. The body memories were present. She cried. She wanted me to make it stop. I couldn't. I reminded her that they were memories of an earlier attempt to reach out. She kept reaching until the body memories subsided.

...Any outside noise or voice startled her, and some frightened her away. At this point in the process, Anne Marie needed more frequent contact. Weekly sessions were increased from one to three, and daily five-minute phone contacts were added. (p. 188)

Changes terrified Anne Marie, as the transference of unpredictable, abandoning Mom and abusive Dad became a part of the therapeutic relationship. After Anne Marie had tested and determined that Audrey cared for her and was there to stay, she became very playful in the sessions and brought in children's storybooks for her therapist to read to her.

Anne Marie is the oldest of four girls. At the age of 5 months, she moved with her parents to another state. The move, Anne Marie was later told, was very traumatic for her as she cried and screamed in terror during the three-day journey. She had been told that she had intractable vertigo and was inconsolable.

One year later, her sister was born setting off rivalry immediately. Her sister could be held and seemed to receive all the parental love that Anne Marie desperately wanted but pushed away. With the birth of two more sisters Anne Marie's wish for parental acceptance, love, recognition, and presence became more faint. Verbal messages were contradictory: "I am here for you, but I can't be" and "You can count on me, but I am too busy." Although she was uncertain as to its onset and frequency, Anne Marie reported being sexually abused by her father until the age of 13.

At 26 she married, believing this to be her salvation from a life of inner isolation. But immediately after the wedding, Anne Marie reported experiencing a recapitulation of the emotional abandonment and abuse of her parent-child relationship. Once again she was alone. She had no real friendships. She stated, "Everyone I let myself get close to, reach out to, leaves . . . hurts me."

Anne Marie quickly replicated the duality of her parental relationship with Audrey. She voiced her need for relationship, but then consistently emotionally distanced herself. At any point of connection she reported shaky feelings as she struggled to control her emerging emotions. She cried, "I don't belong anywhere." And she reported feeling very young, "like an infant." For a while she stopped talking. She had no words. She was angry that Audrey sat across from her like an authority figure who could control her. She became extremely critical and verbally harsh with herself. She coiled her adult body into a small ball—a fetal position—and cried. Anne Marie's silent sobs came from deep within her, a place unfamiliar to both of them at the time. Between sessions, she phoned feeling "panicked, trapped, and in terror." Her anxiety grew as she came to the office.

> She was afraid of the unknown and so was I, but for
> different reasons. She did not know what to do with the

infusion of emotions she was having or how to make sense of her regressed state, and I was intensely afraid of the parental transference that was being established. At this point in the process, I became cognizant that we were working with psychotic or Organizing elements in the transference that were unpredictable. Was I safe? Was she safe? Words fail to fully describe the terror experienced by both parties in the primitive transference—countertransference relationship. (p. 192)

Anne Marie's initial anxiety in coming to Audrey's office was intense. Attempts to contain her anxiety through deep breathing and making herself comfortable on the couch resulted in an influx of strong emotions and a cascading regression. Anne Marie grew aware of these unidentified, fused emotions, and attempted to get away from them—to detach. She described feelings of numbness in her hands and an intense need to get away. This, she said, was the way she felt when her father had come into her room at night. Now she wanted to flee from Audrey as the father she could not get away from. She had many body memories. She felt physical pain. "Audrey, what's happening to me?" She became totally numb physically and reported being mentally lost. Audrey reports feeling helpless to ease the pain even as she worked hard to reassure Anna Marie that she was not in fact being abused, that she was Audrey and not Father. But headlines raced through her head. "Client Accuses Therapist of Sexual Abuse." How easily blurred the boundary between the memories of the past and the present transference reality can become. Audrey understood it was important for Anne Marie to contact the abusive father who lived within, and through the transference to experience her therapist as him abusing her. "It felt awful to watch and experience Anne Marie's pain, and to feel like the perpetrator. I was relieved at the end of the session. I was emotionally drained." Anne Marie was also emotionally drained. Unable to move or drive, she lay in the next office for about two hours before leaving.

The above episode opened the door to a whole new way of doing therapy. Anne Marie grew relentless in her challenges and demands, as she felt certain that she was on the right track. In the next session she reported feeling "broken, alone, isolated, and physically cold." She asked Audrey to sit beside her on the couch and to hold her. Audrey responds, "It's much more comfortable in my chair across from you. What you need and what is comfortable for me in my professional posture are not the same." Later Audrey realizes that Anne Marie was asking for her to be physically near, to be real, to be present. "While I understood the need therapeutically, it felt as if she had asked me to step out on a plank that dangled over a bottomless pool of gurgling lava. I sat next to her and she appeared to have moments of what I thought at the time seemed to be dissociation. I later came to understand these times as moments of interpersonal disconnection which were brought about by her longing for and/or achieving intimate contact."

Audrey's physical presence during her disconnections helped to ground Anne Marie to the present, but triggered Audrey's own childhood asthmatic condition. She struggled to breathe. She wanted to get away. Anne Marie was too close. *The more she reached out for me, the more difficult it was for her and for me to stay emotionally present.* We were both terrified of connecting."

Anne Marie also seemed to treasure any personal information she learned about her therapist. Initially, Audrey was concerned and felt uncomfortable about disclosing personal information. This was not her usual mode of operating.

> However, as she and I moved toward connection, I realized that, as with any healthy relationship, her questions developed out of genuine interest and a need to know rather than entitlement. One question was about my birthday. She remembered the month as a result of leftover items from a staff celebration last year, but did not know the day. Initially, when she asked, I declined to tell her. She accepted my choice but could not hide the hurt. She gave me a birthday card and a little flowerpot (quite symbolic in our work) for my desk. She wanted to celebrate my birthday as it was important to her—I was important to her. Eventually, I shared my birth date and took in her care for me. I took her in and became more vulnerable to her. She, in turn, was able to take me in and connect with me at a much deeper level of relatedness. (p. 195)

As the two moved toward more relatedness, Anne Marie continued to regress. She emotionally and verbally reached out for Audrey, then pushed her away. Audrey interpreted her terror in making the connection. Sometimes she sat curled up on the couch with her head buried in a blanket that she wrapped protectively around herself. At other times she placed the pillows around herself to form a barricade. As memories of her father plagued her, incidents of bingeing and purging became a therapeutic issue. Her regressions initially took the form of an angry teen, a helpless child, and then a terrified infant. Audrey sat next to her to help her stay present.

> Her request for physical contact, for hugs at the end of the sessions and/or to be held, was another crisis point in our

work. Throughout my training, I have taken a conservative position about touch. My position grew out of my desire to stay far away from anything that could be misconstrued by a client. However, the more I learned about individuals working in the Organizing level of development, the more I learned about the potential therapeutic value of touch. My hesitation and cautions, although well-founded and appropriate, slowed her regression work. Anne Marie responded to my hesitation with anger. She felt rejected. She and I had many talks about the therapeutic purpose of touch, which was solely to help her stay present. She read, signed, and discussed an informed consent contract regarding the use of touch in the therapeutic process (see appendices, Hedges 1994c, and 2013e). Overall, she felt that touch helped her to stay present, to know that she was not alone, and that someone cared.

Holding her hand, allowing her to rest her head on a pillow in my lap, allowing her to lean on me, holding her and/or giving her a hug during or at the end of our sessions, would convey my presence more than my words. On one occasion, I denied her a hug as it seemed that her desire was less to stay in contact and more to soothe bad feelings that arose in the session. I wanted her to know that I was still there, and that she did not have to get rid of her bad feelings. (pp 195-6)

Over time, Anne Marie became more aware that her longings and needs were not bad, but that the perceived or actual injuries that she experienced in her initial reaching out to satisfy her needs caused her to recoil and emotionally split off, and to detach her emotional self. As she reached, body memories became more painful. She would scream, most often without sound and sometimes with screeching cries, whimpering, and intense sobbing. She would twist and turn her body, pushing an unseen something from her face, wiping her face, kicking or recoiling into a ball, barricading herself with the pillows on the couch, pulling the blanket tight around her—covering every inch, and then end suddenly in a frozen state. She was unable to move, breathe, or swallow. When her eyes would open, they were empty. She was gone.

Once Audrey realized that these body memories were representations of her past traumas and *serving the internalized psychotic mother who kept her from connections*, Audrey would talk more to her during these times and/or hold her hand so that she could feel her presence.

> The internalized psychotic mother is described by Hedges (1994c) as the internalized representation of the traumatizing other experienced during early attempts to connect. I talked, in part because I felt helpless and wanted her to know that I was there, and also because Anne Marie, when she was able, asked me to keep talking. Talking and holding her hands or her, she reported later, helped her to maintain her awareness of me and facilitated brief moments of connection. (p. 197)

Finally, in one session, the terror in the connection stopped for a few minutes. Anne Marie had asked for and had been granted permission to lean on Audrey's shoulder. She exhaled and settled. She had allowed herself to be emotionally held. Both knew it. She felt small—an infant. It was peaceful. It felt wonderful. She left the office that day with a borrowed teddy bear as she attempted to hold on to that place in which she found the (m)other.

The transference relationship with mother included feelings of betrayal, distance, unpredictability, and "never being there" or "being there but not there." In addressing these issues inherent in the transference, Audrey observed her resistance to taking in the good and in allowing herself to be emotionally comforted by it. She began to use infant analogies more frequently. Audrey described her as a colicky baby who was fussing and kicking so much that she was unaware of mother's presence, or that she was being held. Given this picture of her, she would attempt to settle herself.

As she settled herself and moved once again toward connection, and then again Anne Marie began to experience what she termed as "strange feelings." Somatic memories intensified. She reported being scared and feeling frozen. The predefensive reactions flight or freeze, were present in her relationship with her parents and were being recapitulated in the therapeutic relationship. Her emotions were very frightening to her. She feared being dependent. After an extraordinary internal battle with the vulnerable, infant self, she allowed herself to regress once more.

She sat on the couch and her adult body behaved in ways characteristic of an infant. She sat with her face turned into the couch, or against Audrey's arm, with movements that resembled rooting. During this phase, her use of the teddy bear was critical in maintaining the connection. Periodically she asked Audrey to spray the teddy bear with her perfume. She had connected though touch, hearing, and now smelling—infant senses.

However this place of safe and trusting connection ended when Audrey informed Anne Marie that she would be unavailable during an upcoming weekend. There was rage, head banging, hitting herself and abusing the teddy bear. She felt she had done something wrong or was bad. She was enraged that she had allowed herself to embrace Audrey and felt responsible for her leaving. In a very small voice from somewhere deep inside her, she pleaded, "Don't leave me." She reluctantly accepted reassurances that it would only be a weekend and that Audrey would be back on Monday.

In subsequent sessions Anne Marie did everything she could to create a breach and Audrey found herself feeling lightheaded, dizzy, and sleepy. In the countertransference she felt guilty for causing such pain.

Anne Marie continued to become more present and began to sustain connection for longer periods of time. The two moved from experiencing only moments of connection to her being able to stay connected and hold on to Audrey for a day at a time. She talked about the good feelings she had in finding and being able to sustain connection. At one point she described her feeling as "joy." It seemed that the more present she became the more difficult it was for her to tolerate any breaks in the process.

When Audrey announced her vacation Anne Marie became frozen with fear. She said that she felt as if she were left out for a truck to run over. In her terror, she asked Audrey not to leave. The body memories, the physical coldness, the all-bad self, and the suicidal ideation all returned in full force. This was a very difficult time for Audrey as she fought being identified with the all-bad mother who abandoned her child when she was needed.

> The professional and personal support system I had established helped me to navigate my way through this

arduous place. Anne Marie withdrew emotionally and challenged me verbally about everything. Initially, she minimized the items given to her as aids to maintain connection with me, as well as a phone call I made and a postcard I sent while I was on vacation. Later, she talked of the importance of the items in my absence, but spoiled her care and need for me through creating a good-bad split between me and the good-bad therapist she worked with during my absence. (p. 206)

Then came the ultimate attempt to stop the process and destroy any connection that was there. Anne Marie violated her verbal agreement not to leave her young daughter at her parents' home. They had agreed that as a state mandated reporter, Audrey would have to report any behavior that would place a child at risk for abuse, particularly with a known offender. Consequently, they had agreed that Anne Marie would not leave her daughter at her parents' home for babysitting or any other purpose.

At first, it seemed that Anne Marie's violation of the agreement was a careless act. But it soon became apparent that she was quite aware of the risk involved. Anne Marie lamented, "This is not like me." It soon became clear that this was an all-out attempt to destroy the connection Audrey had with her infant self. Anne Marie—the infant self—was connecting with Audrey, and the internalized psychotic parent was summoned to stop it at any cost as the memories and trauma associated with father were being relived in the transference.

Audrey somewhat reluctantly filed the required abuse report and she and Anne Marie continued to process the terror she felt in connecting that very vulnerable, needy part of herself with Audrey.

This seemed to have been a turning point to a deeper level of processing. Thereafter Anne Marie's dreaming became more regular and reflected her internal life—her searching, her struggle, her needs, her fears, and her truth. The following is an excerpt from one of her dreams:

> I want to bathe but don't want to take off my clothes or towel—they are staring and I can tell they mean me harm—appear nice but the comments and body language tell me to stay away.... Then a door opens and a pregnant woman comes out, the women are mean and threaten her—tell her to go back and do what they tell her if she doesn't want to get hurt—she goes back and continues to wipe the shower down with paper towels—comes back to them—it's not good enough, then they want something else done—nothing is ever going to please them—I can feel they aren't going to let her go—suddenly she balks—doesn't do what they want and they grab her and take a long broom-like stick and shove it inside her—I'm terrified—I know she'll lose her baby.
>
> Then I am in another place with others around and there is a woman having a baby—but it's too young—it's too small—I know it is—I hear someone say "We can try to save it"—but I know it's too little—could hold it in one hand—the mother—something is happening with her—her mouth—surgery? repairing it? The baby is held up and then gone ... (p. 208)

Anne Marie's dream, an internalization of her childhood realities, reflected the lack of safety in her internal world. It identified a world marked by threats, penetration, attempted abortion, and a life-and-

109

death struggle to survive. She feared that the self that she is giving birth to, that vulnerable part of herself, was too small—too young to survive. *She had always lived in constant and terrifying dread that she was going to die. At last her deepest fear of being connected was represented in the dream as well as the transference, that if she stays connected her nascent self is going to abort and die.*

> "Anne Marie taught me that she is the master of her ship, the creator of her futu*re,* and I, much like a parent, simply provide and maintain a healthy and safe environment for her to grow in—to metamorphose into the fully functioning being that she was meant to be."[26]

In all of these case illustrations it seems that some kind of third interpersonal or intersubjective force is behind the scenes making the deep therapeutic work possible. How do we conceptualize and work with this third force that has its roots in the unknown and unknowable? Therapists may wish to go to Appendix D for a thumbnail history of thirds in psychotherapy before going ahead to the next case that illustrates how Thomas Ogden makes use of "the analytic third".

———

## "I've Never Met Anyone Like You Before"— Thomas Ogden[27]

To illustrate how Ogden uses reverie that taps into the speaking third, Ogden relates parts of two sessions with Ms. S, a woman in her late 30's who has been in an intense analysis with him for many years. Before the first session, he hears her using the restroom, which reminds him of an experience they had shared together five years previously in another office. He sadly remembers how empty that office had felt after the death of his office partner. In session, Ms. S recounts a lengthy dream in which she is in his office with him and one of her friends. They are viewing some statues or talismans representing feelings, including one with growing grass (her growth and fertility?, thinks Ogden). In the dream there is reference to an old habit of swimming in an ice-covered lake (her previous coldness and distance?). At the end of the dream, she leaves his office with her friend feeling resigned that she is now able to have friends in life but not a love relationship with a man (she doesn't know how to relate to Ogden as a man?).

We can see as this session begins that Ogden is already having a series of associations to which he is sensitive, though he has no idea what is brewing in them. During the time Ms. S is relating the dream and her associations to it, Ogden reports feeling quite off-balance, having many associations to the dream but feeling them flat, and so choosing to remain silent. He finds his mind wandering to a patient he would be seeing later in the day who is in a great deal of pain and turmoil. Ms. S discusses her fear over the past few weeks of driving in the rain, because she can't see out the windshield well and fears a head-on collision. Ogden's reverie takes him to his older son from New York, who will be arriving in a few days for a visit, and how irritated he is that he has to remind his grown son to meet in the baggage-claim area. This reminds him of having flown with this son to visit his seriously ill father and feeling that it was the two of them who were dying rather than his father. He remembers feeling sad that it was coming to the time that his son would be leaving home. All of this, of course, happens in a flash as the therapy session moves forward. However, by this point in his professional development,

Ogden has learned to neglect none of it, even though he has no idea what this information (from the third) may imply. Ms. S comments that today she did not fold up the blanket on the couch to go under her head to relieve some back discomfort, because then her voice comes from her throat rather than the fuller voice from her chest that she enjoys more. She wonders if he has noticed the difference, and then wonders why she needs such reassurance from him—like in former days. Quickly making use of his reveries, Ogden says: "I suggested that she might be afraid that if she were to feel that she has become a person in her own right and not simply a carrier of parts of me, it would mean not only that the analysis would come to an end, but that we would lose all connection with one another in an absolute way, almost as if one or the other of us had died" (p. 97).

We can see again how in a flash Ogden has integrated his reverie with her dream of leaving the session and her questioning why she needs reassurance from him at this point in her analysis, into a comment on what is invisibly going on between the two of them; that is, that they are slowly and jointly moving toward a separation, an ending of the analysis. Deeply moved by his comment, Ms. S cries, and later in the session says how grateful she feels that he has talked to her in the way he has today, and also for her ability to talk with him in her own way. She states that she doesn't want to say more in the remaining minutes of the session for fear of crowding out what she is feeling (a rich sense of longing and sadness) with space-filling words.

During the remaining quiet time, Ogden experiences a quiet feeling of love for her that he had not previously experienced. It has a sadness about it, as he becomes appreciative of Ms. S's unconscious effort in this session to teach him by showing him the struggle (her with him, and Ogden with his son) in which both of them are engaged, "a struggle to live with the sadness and loss and pride and excitement and sheer inevitability of movement toward separateness that is inherent in growing up and becoming a person in one's own right" (p. 98). In respecting Ms. S's call for a quiet ending for the session, Ogden doesn't share this last observation with her, but we can see he is listening to the invisible third and that he will use this information in the next meeting with her.

The following session begins with Ms. S saying, "'I've never met anyone like you before.'" He laughs, and she joins him. The laughter feels full of mutual affection. Ogden says, "'Maybe you felt that you met me for the first time in yesterday's session. Meeting me in that way is not the same as having a meeting with me'" (p. 98). Psychotherapists often fear that when their minds wander in session, it is due to some personal preoccupation not relevant to the immediate task of therapeutic listening. Ogden has great faith in our unconscious processes and the speaking third. Thus, he allows his mind to wander as it will, and then to focus and use what comes up as part of listening to the third person in the relationship, which informs him of where he and his client are together. In the above example, we can see how his associations lead him to want to hold on to their past relationship (i.e., the prior bathroom incident), to be irritated and sad with his son who is growing up (i.e., as she imagines leaving her analysis some day), to feel sadness over his father's death (i.e., his losing her) and to want to hold on to her former need for him (i.e., his thoughts about his other client in pain). Ogden sees that his client's dream is about her mixed feelings over her growing sense of development and separateness in the relationship—fears of growing into mature triangular relationships and holding her own independent identity against social demands.[28]

113

Although this brief recap fails to do justice to Ogden's rich published clinical illustration, it captures his point that whatever is formulated or realized in the mind of each relating partner surely reflects the evolving process of the analytic third—the processes of the therapeutic relationship.

# Realizing Traumas in Interpersonal/Relational Therapy—Donnel Stern

I had the rare opportunity and pleasure to respond to a case presentation given at the Newport Psychoanalytic Institute on March 16, 2013 by Donnel Stern. The case of William is to appear in his "Relational Freedom" chapter of his forthcoming book (in press). Here are my remarks on the case.

Don, let's examine the material you have presented in your work with William, searching, as always, for transference and countertransference themes, dissociations, and enactments that might be limiting his and/or your relatedness flexibility or, in your terms, relational freedom. Over the time you have spent with William he tells you about and enacts with you his "symbiotic false self compliance scenario" learned in relation to a self-centered mother who expects to be mirrored in her narcissistic grandiosity by his appreciation and gratitude—though his compliance is fraught with bitter resentment. This early symbiotic mode or scenario was transferred—not necessarily inappropriately—by William onto his equally, we are told, narcissistic father.

"Symbiotic scenario" is a term coined in this particular listening perspective to denote the *internalized relational template* or *implicit object relations fantasy* operative at this preverbal level of awareness and being *"replicated"—actually lived out or enacted in emotionally significant relationships, including the transference-countertransference intersubjective field* (Hedges 1983, 1992, 2005).

Through a role-reversal—one endemic to replicated symbiotic relational templates or scenarios—William insists on selfobject appreciation and gratitude from his wife as well as his analyst, (and, like his own parents, no doubt in muted ways from his own three children). But unlike what we expect in the Selfobject listening perspective William is unable to benefit from empathic mirroring either from his wife Jan or you. Rather, William's family and analyst are compulsively assigned the reciprocal role from his family of origin of remaining emotionally distant or standoffish. Other features of the symbiotic listening perspective discernible in the material presented include (1) the splitting of affects when compliance with the scenario is or is not being achieved in the transference; (2) chronic limitations in ego capacities—in William's case debilitating anxieties in the area of social and romantic relations; and (3) personal identity development that is limited largely to work-related preoccupations.

And so Don, you welcome and engage William and you two await the expectable, necessarily unconscious, split off, dissociated aspects of transference-countertransference replications as they fall into place. Over time the analyst and patient alert each other to experiencing and then to the perceiving of various aspects of their replicated interactional scenarios.

As you have so well observed, it's only a matter of time before an adversarial emotional atmosphere develops in the interpersonal field at

115

the symbiotic level of relatedness complexity. "What's going on here anyway? Something is wrong here; something must be done to straighten matters out." For this reason, I have spoken of countertransference as the "royal road to understanding the symbiotic replication experience" (1983, 1992).

First, as therapists we find ourselves in the role of the early parents—some aspect of our analytic relatedness subtly *replicates or re-enacts* the damaging influences known in early childhood. But then we also find ourselves in a role-reversal—experiencing in the countertransference the emotional life of the infant self of our patient, passively experiencing the misattunement and abuse foisted upon us by our patient's unwitting identification with his symbiotic (m)other.

Over time, through countertransference responsiveness, the confrontation slowly forms in our minds and bodies: "This has got to stop, I refuse to take any more of this misunderstanding and maltreatment. You are not relating to *me*! Subtext: "I'm only hired help and I have shown you that I can do it your way, the way you learned relatedness in early childhood. But as Exhibit A of other kinds of relationships in the world, you can't be this way and get away with it. You've got to stop this crappy way of engaging people and pay attention to who each important person in your life really is! The buck stops here!"

Now, of course, we never say any of this directly because the countertransference frustration is always heavily imbued with our own ways of experiencing exasperating interpersonal situations. But we do have to trust our feelings, our sense of our own being, our sense of our own individuated selves. *Our confrontation is not us confronting our clients, or even us confronting their behavior*—our

116

confrontation must be carefully aimed at the emotional template or symbiotic scenario that each client brings to the interpersonal field.

And so we struggle to survive in the morass we are being handed. We struggle to formulate what's going on. We consult with colleagues trying to sort out countertransference in the narrow, personal sense from countertransference that might be usable in the broader interpersonal field to enhance mutual relatedness. We know we have been snared in our own enactments, but we aren't exactly sure just how this is happening; understanding will require an intersubjective engagement, which—as the professional in the room— we must begin.

We sense the moment to strike is coming—the moment to confront what's happening between us, the moment to "stand against" the scenario being haplessly foisted upon us, the moment to stand up for ourselves in all this fray!

Don, you tell us with hindsight that for several weeks before this session you had somehow sensed something big coming, through you were not quite sure what or how. Also, with hindsight you can see that William entered this hour with some fresh openness which you must have unconsciously perceived—you begin the hour with, "One day William arrived for his session in a state of extreme upset." Neither you nor William was consciously aware of the nature of the upset or of the openness to new experience you both sensed was present—you from your curiosity and he from his extreme upset. Something huge was about to happen and you both sensed it.

So William launches into the upsetting spat he had had with his wife the evening before. In adversarial mode, you lie in wait watching the minutes tick by, waiting for your opportunity to take advantage of what you unconsciously perceive as a new vulnerability. You run down your countertransference checklist to be sure that whatever you are about to do truly feels like it's for William and not just for you. Your sword is drawn and, with time quickly running out, you quickly strike! "Maybe you should have called me." Tears, relief, gratitude. William is run-through, pierced to the heart with love. "Maybe you should have called me."

In the aftermath of the moment, it occurs to you that in all the years of hospitals and recovery from his horrible life-threatening automobile accident in college William never once called out for a witness, for someone to recognize his pain, discouragement, and fear, for someone to be emotionally dependent and vulnerable with, for a *Partner in Thought*. Life-shattering sobs ensue—the spell of the symbiosis has been broken. A transformation in "O" has occurred.

In the role-reversal countertransference we could say that you spoke what William as a child could never speak to his parents. "Mother, in all of your narcissistic loneliness *you should have called me*—called on me to be your beautiful baby whom you could grow through by nurturing, reflecting, and witnessing my developing being." "Father, you could have escaped your self-imposed isolation and frail sense of manliness if you had just called on me your beautiful, God-given son, to reflect your own proud fathering. But you did not call. Instead, you taught me not to be vulnerable, not to know my own dependency, not to call out for help in growing." And then follows the *piece de resistance* of the hour, the precipitating morning event with his wife and children turning their backs and leaving William behind—the event that triggered William's opening extreme upset and signaled to you a new openness was available and at last an opportunity for you to "stand against" his lifelong scenario or emotional isolation and pain.

Simultaneous with William's emotional break-through, you let us know that your part of the mutual enactment broke. Your confrontation of William's scenario that you had been hooked into for so long— "Maybe you should have called me"—came from a deep sense of *me, myself, and I*, from a deep sense of *what's right for me if I'm allowed to be a real person in this relationship*.

*In one passionate adversarial moment two people experienced transformation in "O", a new degree of relational freedom. "Maybe you should have called me." "Maybe you should have called me."*

# Conclusions

Experiences of somatic and psychic trauma are universal and normal. Moreover, trauma is essential to our mental and physical growth and well-being. Through processes of assimilation and accommodation we receive disturbing stimulation from within and from without that helps us grow and expand to meet the challenges of life. Traumatic experiencing forces us to continuously reevaluate and re-organize our current body-, mind-, and relationship-sets.

Since ancient Greece trauma has been understood as the processes of recovering from overwhelming and disintegrating stimulation. But activities aimed at recovering, regrouping, and realigning our bodies and minds leave their mark—a scar as it were, to commemorate the event.

The cumulative effect of trauma continuously experienced during the course of growing up and living a robust life is a set of somatic and psychic constrictions and somatic contractions that curtail our liveliness, threaten our health, and limit the richness of our relationships as well as our longevity.

In human life the greatest source of overwhelming stimulation is from needed relationships that have broken down or somehow failed to protect us from overwhelming stimulation—whether with family, friends, colleagues, or society. We rise to the occasion, struggle to meet the challenge, and fight to stem the tide. When we have been able to successfully assimilate the intrusive simulation we feel relieved, reinforced, and strengthened. But when our efforts to accommodate to internal or external demands falter or fail our bodies contract and our mental relational extensions constrict. A sign is posted somewhere inside, "never reach that way again".

A century of psychoanalytic study has yielded an understanding of our relational development and the kinds of fears that accompany us at each stage of relational differentiation. Seven relational fears have been defined on a developmental continuum that haunt the simplest relationships to the most complex. The seven relational fears arise from disturbing demands placed on us during the course of normal and expectable growing up—and in the course of normal, expectable relationships. Each of us carries in our mind and body a set of primary constrictions and contractions—fear reflexes—that serve to limit our full relatedness potentials.

Sigmund Freud was the first to discover that our unconscious patterns of internalized constrictions and contractions could be experienced, re-lived, and released in the context of a safe and intimate therapeutic relationship. At the time they were formed, our fear reflexes were appropriate in helping us survive or even thrive in a certain relational setting. However, later in life those same patterns of constriction and restriction no longer serve us in other relational settings. This is Freud's essential definition of psychoneurosis—which we now understand to be the normal state of human beings.

Trauma and its psychological aftermath have always been understood to be at the heart of mental distress. But it was Freud who first grasped that the *therapeutic* focus needed to be not on the intrusive event or the narrative surrounding the overwhelming and disintegrating experience itself, but rather on the ways that each person has assimilated and accommodated—that is, internalized and identified with—the source and meaning of the intrusive stimulation.

Over the last three decades somatic and psychic trauma and their after-effects have become the subject of serious multidisciplinary study. At first being viewed as medical disorders, a veritable cottage industry has grown up around the identification and amelioration of extreme forms of "post-traumatic stress disorders" (PTSD). Closer scrutiny, however, reveals that trauma and post-traumatic experience (PTE) are a universal and normal part of human development and merit attention whether they are the ordinary and expectable cumulative traumas of normal life or more extreme forms of stress and focal traumas.

Interpersonal/Relational Psychotherapy addresses the traumas and the constrictive and contractive effects of post-traumatic experience in body, mind, and relationship. While there are many ways that the effects of trauma can be ameliorated, because trauma exists in cumulative forms that span an entire lifetime of relational experiences, an in-depth therapeutic relational experience of systematically studying and re-living those traumas (in transference, resistance, and countertransference) is required to fully release the constrictions and contractions in the service of attaining greater relatedness flexibility and freedom.

# Appendices for Psychotherapists

This book is primarily written to a general audience of people interested in thinking about and resolving cumulative developmental traumas.

For readers who are psychotherapists and may wish more theoretical background I have created four appendices as follows:

Appendix A
The Formation of Character and Character Armor

Appendix B
Epistemology and the Creation of Relational Listening Perspectives

Appendix C
Some Features of Interpersonal/Relational Psychotherapy

Appendix D
A Thumbnail History of Thirds in Interpersonal/Relational Therapy

I hope you find these helpful.

*Appendix A*

# The Formation of Character and Character Armor

The subject of mind-body relational reaching and its consequences have been considered in ways by different researchers and practitioners. Psychologist Carl Shubs reviews the work of the psychoanalyst Wilhelm Reich(1942, 1945), the bioenergetic analyst Robert Hilton (1977, 2007), and his own somatic/relational psychotherapy in a *tour de force* on the topic of developmental trauma in his forthcoming book, *Traumatic Experiences of Normal Development: An Intersubjective, Object Relations Listening Perspective on Self, Attachment, Trauma, and Reality (in press)*. Following are four diagrams from Shubs' work, which I will explain.

Figure 1 depicts Wilhelm Reich's original formulation of how somatic and psychic defensive character armor is formed. As the reaching hand (arrow) encounters a relational obstacle, somatic and psychic defensive structures constituting what Reich calls "character armor" are gradually built to protect oneself from further disappointing and painful intrusive traumas from others.

In Figure 2 Robert Hilton modifies Reich's formulation to further depict how *the "no" becomes internalized in one's personality to thwart future reaching*, and how a creatively adaptive ego structure is constantly generated in an attempt to reach out again in a different, safer way.

In Figure 3 Carl Shubs adapts Reich's and Hilton's prior diagrams to indicate that character armor is being continuously built at the same time that the internalized "no" or internal impediment is developing.

The external as well as internalized relational obstacles force the creative ego to build and to try to get around both the defensive character armor and the internalized "no".

In Figure 4 Shubs extends his prior diagram to indicate that at each relational block the reaching person's creative ego attempts again to get around the block so that the structure of the ego becomes more and more complex and defensively internalized with every step of development. Donald Winnicott has called this process the development of the "false self"(1965).

These formulations, on the one hand, indicate the ways that a person's healthy adaptive, creative ego can be gradually built out of optimal frustrations. On the other hand, however, severe frustrations or obstacles may well produce counter-productive internalized somatic and psychic defensive "character armor" that will severely limit one's relational reaching in the future—that is, a strong internalized inhibiting "no" will stop the reaching so that the fundamental life-giving impulse to reach out in order to benefit from new relational learning experiences becomes stymied. Elsewhere, I have spoken of the result of this process as a sign being posted in one's neurological system that reads "never reach that way again (1994a, b)."[29]

These diagrams illustrate the way the promise of life can slowly, safely, and confidently be realized through optimal frustrations that can be slowly assimilated. They also illustrate the way that the promise of life can become inhibited, constricted or even crushed by the way one traumatically accommodates to and cumulatively internalizes overwhelming relational obstacles. Note here that we are talking about psychic constrictions as well as somatic contractions—and that ongoing inhibitions in both psyche and soma are inextricably bound to traumatically experience intimate personal relationships.

Hedges' Seven Deadly Fears (2013c,d) are briefly summarized in the present text and then systematically applied to the case illustration to demonstrate how primary traumas produce mental and physical inhibitions that heavily determine how later interpersonal relational experiences—secondary trauma—are perceived and experienced.

*Appendix B*
# Epistemology and the Creation of Relational Listening Perspectives[30]

Something in us wants certainty, demands the best possible fix on reality, experiences discomfort unless we know for sure, insists on finally knowing "the truth" of what's really out there—the so-called "modern" perspective. Psychoanalytic theorizing, like the theorizing that preceded it in the natural and social sciences, has followed this unyielding human demand for certainty into the pursuit of "the true nature of mind"—even though at this point in time it is widely understood that objective certainty, as it has been sought in science is, in principle, an impossibility —the "post-modern perspective." The result is that the psychoanalytic enterprise, after a century of clinical experience and theoretical elaboration, is an ever-expanding, tangled labyrinth of competing and contradictory truths and myths emanating from any number of schools of thought—each religiously purporting in its own way to have a corner on the truth of mental functioning. Lost in the burgeoning body of psychotherapeutic and psychoanalytic work, however, has been the essential epistemology and philosophy of science informing 20th-century thought that reveals the traditional approach to knowledge expansion to be anachronistic and untenable. The same generalization can be said for the vast trauma literature—it is hopelessly based on discovering the truths about trauma and developing ways to address those truths.

When we think of traumatic experiences we know that they can and do exist at all developmental stages of human growth. But what is experienced as overwhelming intrusive stimulation differs from child to child, person to person, contextual moment to contextual moment and developmental stage to developmental stage.

In my 1983 book *Listening Perspectives in Psychotherapy,* I set out to reformulate a century of psychoanalytic psychology along lines that are more compatible with a contemporary "postmodern" epistemology and philosophy of science—with the hope of liberating psychotherapeutic theory and practice from an obsolete 19th-century "modern" scientific paradigm. At this point in time that same epistemological approach needs to be applied to the study of the seven universal developmental fears and how they produce trauma.

My ongoing studies have reorganized the central concepts of psychotherapeutic practice—transference, resistance, and countertransference—along the lines of *listening to progressively more complex internalized self-and-other relationship possibilities.* This epistemological move makes it possible to conceptualize an infinite set of individualized patternings of relational possibility that can be reconstellated in an endless variety of ways in the context of every psychoanalytic relationship. In trauma study the listening perspective approach offers this same wide expansion of possibilities. With the potential data pool thus expanded to an infinity of relational possibilities comparable to the expanded data pool of the other 20th-century postmodern sciences, questions can then be entertained as to what perspectives on the forever elusive data of mind one might choose to define at any moment in time, and for what purposes.

## Listening Perspectives as Frames for Understanding Relational Experience

The Listening Perspectives approach as I have defined it and others have adopted it, aids in framing for therapeutic understanding different qualities of internalized interpersonal relatedness experience as they arise in the here-and-now cognitive-emotional-motivational matrix of the therapeutic relationship. Based on the work of the philosophers Wittgenstein (1953), Ryle (1949), Rorty (1989), and Searle (2005), this philosophical and epistemological orientation has been elaborated further in light of quantum and chaos theories (Hedges 1992) and seeks to mitigate against ever assuming or proceeding as if we know or understand with certainty anything that's "really there." This approach represents a radical shift in the conception and perception of the interpersonal relatedness experience itself that is seldom fully appreciated and has massive implications for the psychotherapeutic study of cumulative developmental traumatic experiences.

The relatedness Listening Perspectives approach abandons entirely the naïve view that we can ever objectively consider how "things really are" or that the human mind can ever be studied as an isolated unit separate from the biophysical, sociocultural, and intersubjective fields in which human beings necessarily live. The perspectival view of truth and reality maintains that all we can ever do with any degree of certainty is to generate systematically helpful points of view, perceptual angles, and/or empathic stances or lenses from which to listen in order to frame (to experience in the broadest possible sense) what people have to tell us and to the ways in which two people engage each other in the here-and-now therapeutic relationship. This way of approaching the psychotherapeutic situation encourages us as professional listeners to experience ourselves as living human participants involved in a full emotional relationship with someone endeavoring to experience, and to express in one way or another, his or her relational life experiences.

The Listening Perspectives approach further encourages us to formulate our work in terms of theories that enhance listening and speaking possibilities within a living, breathing, here-and-now relationship, rather than theories that seek to reify or personify concepts or to capture the eternal verities of existence or the true nature of the human mind as objectively defined and viewed in isolation. This approach finds fault with all reified and personified processes—including multiple selves, dissociation, and enactments.

The four self-and-other relational Listening Perspectives to be briefly considered here have evolved out of more than 100 years of psychoanalytic research that bridge across existing theories of the mind.

## The Four Relational Listening Perspectives

The number and ways of defining Listening Perspectives from which to study the transactions of relational encounters is entirely open-ended and arbitrary. But a century of psychoanalytic study suggests four distinctly different relational Listening Perspectives that have served the purpose of framing self-and-other intersubjective relatedness patterns that operate in the interpersonal field (or, differently said, the constructions arising from the transference-countertransference or intersubjective matrix). Traditional "modern" scientific-objective approaches pre-specify in various ways *the presumed nature* of psyche, what kinds *of structures and contents* an analytic observer is likely to see, and the ways in which the analytic search for *transference and resistance memories* are best framed. This same approach to "knowing" is also true for most approaches to trauma study. That is, the trauma literature is replete with clear definitions, narratives, and procedures that are based upon the presumed realities of traumatic and posttraumatic experience. A more intersubjective-relational listening perspective approach simply defines an array of human relatedness possibilities that could serve to frame, for mutual understanding, *whatever* idiosyncratic narratives and narrational interactions emerge for mutual observation in the course of the relationship development.

Internalized relatedness patterns from the lived past of each participant, as well as novel configurations emerging from the intersubjective engagement of therapy will be an expectable focus of discussion as the therapeutic relationship unfolds (Hedges, 1983, 1992, 1996, 2000b, 2013e, 2013f). Emotional honesty and limited disclosure of affective experience on the part of the analyst will be an expectable part of the emerging therapeutic relationship (Aron 1996, Maroda 1999). The development of a personal creative style of relating that integrates, like postmodern art, a variety of ideas and interventions into the specific therapeutic exchange will be another expectable aspect of the emergent dialogue (Johnson 1991). A multiplicity of ways of viewing and working together with the internalized patterns of both people, and the emerging configurations of interactions characteristic of the couple, can also be expected (Stark 1994, 1997, 2015).

The four Listening Perspectives that follow are based on developmental *metaphors* of how a growing child potentially engages and is engaged by emotionally significant others in interpersonal interactions that build internal habits, structures, or patterns of relational expectation. Understanding the general sequence of human relational development allows an understanding of how primary trauma provides the basis for how any subsequent traumatic incident or secondary trauma is likely to be experienced. Differential framing of each metaphoric level of self and other experience secures for therapeutic study the *structures, patterns, configurations,* and/or *modes* of internalized interpersonal interaction that have characterized

131

the past interactions of both participants and that are transferred into and resisted conscious awareness and expression in the current mutually developing psychotherapeutic relationship.

Listening Perspectives thus formed do *not* represent a developmental schema, but rather serve to identify a general array of relatedness possibilities lived out each day by all people. Careful study of the Developmental Listening Charts (of which I and II follow) reveals a general coherency of approach.

*The central idea here is that if we want to empathically engage with a child or a person re-experiencing some pattern of reactions or traumatic adaptations learned in childhood, we have to understand the relatedness level currently in play and respond in kind.* For example, an infant may grasp the emotional intent of a speaking adult but the content is essentially incomprehensible. On the other hand, if we speak to an older child or adult as if they were much younger they are likely to feel infantilized, angered, or insulted. It follows that if a therapeutic strategy depends on shifting cognitions, setting goals, and/or attaining insight when the relatedness patterns, the internalized traumatic adaptations, are currently operating at a much less complex emotional level, then the results of the therapy process will simply be an intellectualized false-self compliance cure rather than relationally transformative.

Furthermore, recall my earlier reference to physicists who tell us that we are actively living in ten or more dimensions while we can only consciously perceive four of them. This means that even the most sophisticated adult formulations only touch the surface of our deeper beings, of the patterns that operate in the unformulated and unformulatable parts of our personalities, and of the possibilities for transformation that exist for us. The British psychoanalyst Wilfred

Bion came to believe that all transformations—whether developmentally formative or therapeutically re-formative—occur at the level of "O"—the dimensions of our existence that are unknown and unknowable! The bottom line: we do not know all of the forces that promote our growth or that can be mobilized in overcoming disintegrative traumatic experiences—but we assume those forces are within us and working for all of us. What we can do, however, is create perspectives from which to listen to our clients in the broadest sense of the word so that whatever internal healing processes are available to a person can be mobilized in transformations that free that person from the bondage of her or his own internalized developmental traumatic adaptations.

Here I can do little more than sketch the features of the Listening Perspectives as they have evolved over the years and are explicated and illustrated more fully in my previous publications. The four perspectives are metaphors describing an array of human relatedness potentials from the simplest to the most complex.[31]The first chart that follows describes the developmental levels of relatedness. Developmental Listening Charts I and II re-describe the same four developmental levels with brief descriptions of features involved in interpersonal/developmental relating in transference, resistance and countertransference. From here we will move to the Seven Deadly Fears.

## The Four Relatedness Listening Perspectives Chart

I. THE ORGANIZING EXPERIENCE: Infants require certain forms of connection and interconnection in order to remain psychologically alert and enlivened to themselves and to others. In their early relatedness they are busy "organizing" physical and mental channels of connection—first to mother's body, later to her mind and to the minds of others—for nurturance, stimulation, evacuation, and soothing. *Framing* organizing patterns for analysis entails studying how two people approach to make connections and then turn away, veer off, rupture, or dissipate the intensity of the connections.

II. THE SYMBIOTIC EXPERIENCE: Toddlers are busy learning how to make emotional relationships (both good and bad) work for them. They experience a sense of merger and reciprocity with their primary caregivers, thus establishing many knee-jerk, automatic, characterological, and role-reversible patterns or scenarios of relatedness. *Framing* the symbiotic relatedness structures entails noting how each person *characteristically* engages the other and how interactive scenarios evolve from two subjectively-formed sets of internalized self-and-other interaction patterns.

III. THE SELFOTHER EXPERIENCE: Three-year-olds are preoccupied with using the acceptance and approval of *others* for developing and enhancing *self*-definitions, *self*-skills and *self*-esteem. Their relatedness strivings use the admiring, confirming, and idealized responses of significant others to firm up their budding sense of self. *Framing* for analysis the self-other patterns used for affirming, confirming, and inspiring the self entails studying how the internalized mirroring, twinning, and idealizing patterns used in self-development in the pasts of both participants play out to enhance and limit the possibilities for mutual self-to-selfother resonance in the emerging interpersonal engagement.

IV. THE INDEPENDENCE EXPERIENCE: Four- and-five-year-olds are dealing with triangular love-and-hate relationships and are moving toward more complex social relationships. In their relatedness they experience others as separate centers of initiative and themselves as independent agents in a socially cooperative and competitive environment. *Framing* the internalized patterns of independently interacting selves in both cooperative and competitive triangulations with real and fantasized third parties entails studying the emerging interaction patterns for evidence of repressive forces operating within each participant and between the analytic couple that work to limit or spoil the full interactive potential.

## Relational Listening Charts I and II

### *Relational Listening I:*
### *Development, Transference, Countertransference*

| Age | Developmental Thrust | Transference | Countertransference |
|---|---|---|---|
| > 3 yrs | Self and other Relational Experiences | From Independent, Ambivalently Held Others | Overstimulating Experiences as Distracting or Impediment |
| 24 to 36 Months | Self-consolidating, Recognition Experiences | From Resonating or Injuring Self – Others | Facilitating Experiences of Fatigue, Boredom, and Drowsiness |
| 4 to 24 Months | Symbiotic and Separating Scenarios/ Interactive Experience | From Interacting and Enacting Others – Replication | Resistive Experiences to Replicating Demanding, Dependent Scenarios |
| ± 4 Months | Organizing Merger and Rupturing Experiences | From Engaging and Disengaging Others | Dread and Terror of Unintegrated Experiences |

## Relational Listening II:
## Resistance, Listening Mode, Therapeutic Intervention

| Age | Resistance | Listening Mode | Therapeutic Intervention |
|---|---|---|---|
| > 3 yrs | To the Return of The Repressed | Evenly Hovering Attention Free Association Equidistance | Interpretive Reflection: Verbal-Symbolic Interpretation |
| 24 to 36 Months | To Experiencing Narcissistic Shame and Narcissistic Rage | Resonance with Self-Affirmation, Confirmation, and Inspiration | Empathic Attunement to Self and Self-Other Resonance |
| 4 to 24 Months | To Assuming Responsibility for Differentiating | Replicating and Renouncing Symbiotic and Separating Scenarios | Replication Standing Against the Symbiotic & Separating Scenarios: Reverberation |
| ± 4 Months | To Bonding Connections and Engagements | Engagement: Connection, Interception; Linking | Focus on and Interception of Disengagements |

# Chart Comparing Four Listening Perspectives with Seven Deadly Fears

| | |
|---|---|
| The Organizing Experience | 1. The fear of being alone |
| | 2. The fear of making connections |
| The Symbiotic Experience | 3. The fear of abandonment |
| | 4. The fear of self-assertion |
| The Self-Other Experience | 5. The fear of being unacceptable |
| The Independent Experience | 6. The fear of failure and success |
| | 7. The fear of being fully alive |

*Appendix C*
# Some Features of Interpersonal/Relational Psychotherapy

## Overview of Relational Psychotherapy and Psychoanalysis

It is not possible here to do justice to what the Interpersonal/Relational Psychotherapy movement is about. But a few summary comments may be helpful.

The essential aspects of the evolving Interpersonal/Relational approach are:

1. *Symmetry* exists between the two separate and equal personal subjectivities that engage each other towards mutual recognition in the intersubjective field of psychotherapy and psychoanalysis. Yet *asymmetry* often characterizes the therapeutic situation as well, since the therapist can be seen as an experienced expert and leader although at times the roles can also switch.

2. The *co-creation* of a mutually achieved rhythm and harmony of emotional relating, and the emergence of a co-constructed set of relational realities evolves in the therapeutic relationship that is rich, complex, and often confusing and contradictory. Mutually engaged ego and self boundaries are in constant flux between fruitful and dangerous interpenetrations.

3. The emergent sense of the importance and reality of *the relationship itself (i.e.,"the therapeutic or analytic third")* can be fruitfully studied by the therapeutic dyad.

4. *Numerous dialectics of personality formation*—for example, oedipal/preoedipal, narcissistic/object love, depressive /manic affect splits, passive/active participation, and masculine/feminine gender attributes—may all be mutually experienced and worked through in the relational context.

5. A full array of *developmentally determined relational patterns* becomes mutually engaged and worked through in the transference/countertransference/resistance aspects of the therapeutic relationship.

6. The concept of isolated minds (our personal psychology) is generally relinquished in favor of minds at all times being engaged with other minds (two-person or intersubjective psychology).[32]

7. *Multiple self-states* and processes of *dissociation* characterize the interpersonal/relational approach. It is assumed that multiple dissociated self-states exist from birth and with good-enough relational experience tend to become integrated into an overall sense of a cohesive unitary self—though many self-states may remain dissociated because they were not positively responded to, i.e. dissociated as "bad-me" or "not-me." When dissociated self states become mutually engaged in co-created relationships the result is mutual non-conscious enactments until one person or the other is able to bring the dissociated states into conscious dialogue.[33]

8. *Internalized personality functions and structures* featuring increased flexibility, expanded horizons, novel possibilities of relating, and relational freedom are thought to emerge from a relationally-centered treatment process

# A Thumbnail History of Thirds in Interpersonal/Relational Therapy

## The Third Person in Relationships

One very important dimension of the Interpersonal/Relational Psychotherapy movement is the discussion of "relational thirds." We have learned more about human nature in the past three decades than we have known since the beginning of time. One of the most stunning insights to emerge from recent psychological research is that every emotionally intimate relationship creates an invisible third presence or intersubjective field—or metaphorically a "third person"—who continuously monitors and informs us about the current state of the relationship.

The running commentary of this invisible third can be attended to in order to carefully track how we and our relating partners are experiencing what transpires within us and between us. More remarkable, it is maintained by many relationists that this presence can exist almost as a third party who "speaks" for the relationship itself. It is thought that we can learn how to tune into this mysterious presence of voice to enrich and preserve our relationships, or we can choose to ignore or deny it to our detriment.

When the study of "thirds" first began in our field twenty years ago, I heavily resisted reifying the idea in order to make what we can't see into a subject of discussion. Nor am I fond of personifying a process—of giving the intangible a set of human attributes. But with time I have seen the utility, both in theory and in practice, of referring loosely to third processes as a "third person" in intimate relating. It is because these third processes in relationships have an uncanny way of developing a life of their own, and of silently telling us and our relating partners who we are and how we are to be with each other. If you are having trouble with the reification (making processes into a thing) and personification (turning a thing into a person), try to suspend your disbelief for a while. And you will come to see what emerges for you in your own understanding and in your own intimate relationships. I think the reason this process is useful is because we are constantly observing and talking to ourselves but not really noticing what that dialogue is about. Imagining a third is speaking to me causes me to be a more critical listener to interpersonal processes I am engaged in.

## The Nature of Psychotherapy Consulting

For forty years I have met daily with groups of therapists to discuss our most difficult casework. Now why, you may ask, would fully trained therapists take the time to huddle with mentoring people like myself just to talk about their clients — aren't they already well trained experts? The answer is that when therapists get to know people deeply and intimately in the privacy of a consulting room, their client's true and often latent or silent selves begin to emerge — as do their own! It's not as simple as clients just telling their therapists secrets they have never told anyone before. Or even saying things they never dared to think about themselves — although that happens all the time. It's that people begin *to actually relate to their therapists* in ways they find puzzling, shocking, shameful, aggressive, lustful, and even self-destructive (i.e., through enactments). And therapists respond with their own, often never before encountered, forms of relatedness (mutual enactments) that are often surprising, dismaying, and even threatening. Over the period of a deepening therapeutic relationship, clients learn to relate openly and spontaneously to their therapists, understanding it is for the purpose of "letting it all hang out," so that deeper invisible parts of themselves can be encountered and known by two. Or in the words of Donnell Stern, so that unformulated dissociated experiences can be mutually enacted (non-consciously) and they can be formulated or *realized* in the relationship.

People in therapy cultivate the attitude of being as natural and spontaneous as possible with their therapists. And relational therapists do their best to be honest and open in the therapeutic relationship as well. As we will come to see, when therapists closely study what's transpiring in their intimate professional relationships, mysterious and invisible forces (thirds) begin to appear which can inform the therapist about what's happening beneath the surface. But it often takes the therapist articulating for expert or peer review the strange experiences she or he is having before the voice of the third person can be discerned. Sounds strange? Indeed, it is.

This is what is so hard for people who haven't been in long-term, intensive therapy to grasp: As therapist and client work toward being as fully candid and spontaneous with one another as possible, a knee-jerk relationship dance develops that becomes a surprise to both. That is, as each begins to know the other better, they can anticipate the other's responses and play to them—consciously and non-consciously. This special, evolving culture of two—their unique ways of being together—soon takes on an existence of its own that has come to be called "the third force (or person or subject) in the relationship" by therapists. This same process can be cultivated in any committed or intimate relationship. That is, relating partners can learn to work together on noticing various thoughts, feelings, and body sensations that seem to "randomly" or "inexplicably" appear in the course of their relationship and also learn to bring up these not quite sensible experiences to each other for mutual consideration. The voice of the mythical third person speaks to us in strange ways, and two can cultivate a mutually sensitive and attentive attitude toward messages from the third with illuminating results.

In describing the therapeutic relationship I haven't mentioned anything that's not true of any really good intimate relationship. Except perhaps the last point—that in Relational Psychotherapy the two deliberately study each new relational element as it appears in the here-and-now. In daily life we rarely take the time to focus on what is happening between you and me right this minute, and how we each feel about it or are reacting to it. Nor have most of us acquired the necessary tools to make such an ongoing joint study illuminating. In understanding our relationships, we don't yet have a full appreciation of how much time, focus, and emotion are truly needed to benefit from being on deeply intimate terms with another person. Nor has our culture come to appreciate the enormous personal benefits that can come from studying spontaneous interactions in intimate relationships.

After studying the psychotherapeutic process for more than a century, we now realize how incredibly complex and unique each one of us truly is. But recent advances in neuroscience and infant research have been able to clarify *why*. It is because *in our earliest relationships, each or our brains are stimulated to develop differently*—to see some things, to ignore others, to value certain interactions, to avoid others, and so on. Mental rhythms, expectancies, and templates are formed in the brain and throughout the neurological system based on emotional-relational experiences occurring in the first months of life. These all influence and guide later development so that each of our developmental paths is indeed totally unique. Our brains bear the imprint of those unique early relationship experiences (relational assimilation and accommodation) of good & bad. Furthermore, during each stage of emotional development, our neuron systems *actually form and change* according to the input we receive from emotional relationships and *structure who we are and who we are to become!*

In later childhood and adulthood, we learn through parenting and school relationships how the world operates and how we are supposed to be and behave. In short, we become culturally conditioned—trained to be what the world around us wants us to be. This training is accomplished through positive and negative relationship experiences growing up. Along the way we assimilate and accommodate relational expectations. True, many of our early character differences survive the later cultural conditioning. But in our immature eagerness to fit in, our true uniqueness tends to get (traumatically) lost in social conformity. Lost, that is, until we enter an intimate relationship when our unique, as well as our less agreeable, less socially-integrated sides begin to present themselves for interaction and possible transformation.

So relationships are not only influential in terms of individual development, they are *everything* in terms of what makes up our private inner selves. Most of us have no difficulty whatsoever pointing to relationships that have been hurtful, embarrassing, shameful, frightening, or damaging. And we know that those strong negative experiences have had an impact on our later capacities to be free, easy, open, and loving in our intimate relationships. Likewise, we can also recall with great clarity moments of emotional bliss, success, gratitude, and triumph—as well as their favorable impact on us and what people facilitated our experiences.

## A Thumbnail History of Psychological Thirds

The earliest record we have of subjectivity and intersubjectivity, according to philosopher Michel Foucault (1985), comes from ancient Greece.[35] Foucault's detailed and scholarly analysis of the structure of Greek, Roman, Middle Ages, Renaissance, and nineteenth-century European societies allows us to understand that it was only through the mentoring relationship among older and younger freeborn (and later aristocratic) men that subjectivity and intersubjectivity as cultural phenomena gradually emerged in Western civilization. Robert Stolorow and his colleagues (Stolorow, Atwood, and Brandchaft 1994) were perhaps the first contemporary psychoanalysts to expose clearly the myth of the isolated mind as they strove to develop a psychoanalysis based on the interpenetration of minds—on the field of the third, or of intersubjective realities. Relational psychoanalysts Stephen Mitchell (1988), Jay Greenberg(1983), Lewis Aron (1991, 2001), Jessica Benjamin (2004, 2010), and others building on the work of Sandor Ferenczi (1955 ) and Harry Stack Sullivan (1953), have forged an international movement among psychotherapists focusing on the relational third variously conceptualized as a force field, a vector, a matrix, or a personified subject in her own right—in short—a third person.

Meanwhile, infant researchers led by Daniel N. Stern (2004) became aware of how complex human mutual cuing and intersubjective emotional processes truly are. It became clear that infants are born with a drive for intersubjective exchanges. The fundamental neurological processes, which govern who we are as individuals and as a species, rely for optimal development on the early emotional exchanges between infant and caregiver. The crucial importance of right brain to right brain mutual emotional regulation between infant and caregiver has been carefully researched by Alan Schore (2013). Further, the third force of infant development has been traced back to many aspects of intrauterine life—perhaps as far as conception with the apparent finding that the egg "chooses" which sperm fertilizes it and that some third force participates in this choice.

Adding further to the complexity and texture of intersubjective thirds is the work of neuropsychologist Steve Porges (2011) and his astounding work on the determining force of polyvagal nerve functioning. The first vagal nerve evolved in reptiles to regulate visceral responses and to insure a set of instantaneous survival responses. Later vagal nerves, which evolved first in mammals, were further refined in primates and began to regulate a series of intersubjective sensitivities involving touch, smell, sound, movement, sight, and taste. The latest polyvagal nerves of humans control all of the facial, ocular, and auricular muscles as well as the pharynx and the larynx; so that, when we engage in social communication, we are actively receiving and transmitting messages into and out of each other's brains. That is, the actual neurons of our social engagement systems are at all times *interpenetrating into each other's central and autonomic nervous systems!* Both Porges and neuropsychologist Alan Schore (2013) as well as many others have established evidence that third forces developing in child-caregiver pairs are genetically driven—that the "third person," passing messages back and forth about the state of the self, the other, and the union, is co-created and develops a life of its own at a social as well as neuropsychological level.

In terms of our learning how to identify and to use information provided by the third person to enhance intimate relationships, Freud as early as 1915 was the first to acknowledge the inevitability of love emerging in the psychoanalytic relationship. Unfortunately, however, the intensity of intimate feelings and the fantasies arising in the psychoanalyst so frightened Freud that he advised only abstinence and more personal analysis designed to keep the analyst "objective."

Despite earlier work by Sandor Ferenczi (1920-33, 1955) and Michael Balint (1930-52 papers, 1985) in Budapest, it was only in London during the 1950's that the loving, intimate feelings—as well as the hateful ones—i.e., the countertransference arising in the analyst first came to be seen as vital information about what was happening in the analytic relationship. (For a review see Hedges 1992) But it was not until the 1980's that the complex feelings of the analyst began to be acknowledged in the work of Christopher Bollas (1987) and to point clearly toward Robert Stolorow and George Atwood's (1992) intersubjective field of experience. My own work in 1983 and 1992 was clear in pointing to the importance of relying on countertransference—the feeling states of the therapist—for relational information in psychotherapy. It was Stephen Mitchell who in 1988, building on the pioneering work of Sandor Ferenczi and Harry Stack Sullivan, boldly formulated a relational way of thinking and working that not only forever liberated psychoanalysis from the myth of the isolated mind, but pointed hopeful directions for intersubjectively understanding and enhancing all of our intimate relationships.

One might go on citing anecdotal data that has been accumulating throughout history in all cultures regarding unusual access to primitive mind-body experiences and how the third force field has molded and shaped these experiences. The bottom line for our purposes is that at last we have the technology to begin studying what factors are at play in our mysterious experiences, and to begin using this new knowledge to enhance our intimate relationships.[36]

## Thomas Ogden's Third Person

The person who to my mind has made the most imaginative and creative use of the intersubjective third is San Francisco psychoanalyst Thomas Ogden. In his book *Conversations at the Frontier of Dreaming* (2002), Ogden shows in a very courageous way how he uses the third in his consulting room every day. In this and previous and subsequent books, Ogden formulates the analytic third as a speaker and endows her with qualities resembling intelligence and speech—*an "analytic subject"*.

Ogden likens therapeutic listening to experiencing poetry rather than the more traditional decoding of hidden meanings. He uses Wilfred Bion's (1962) definition of reverie as daydreams, fantasies, ruminations, and bodily sensations that arise in the course of therapeutic relating and represent unconscious meanings—messages from the analytic third, as it were. I have taken a similar position in several of my own books that illustrate in numerous cases such listener responsiveness as reported by a number of different therapists. (1992, 1994a,b, 1996, 2000b) In context each therapist demonstrates that, *when both partners work on realizing and representing the actual relating process itself as it is taking place, the results are illuminating and mutually transformative.*

# Notes

— [1] Unfortunately, Freud's point of view became widely misunderstood as if he had said that the event itself was not important. Freud never said any such thing. He knew full well that the specifics of the intrusive event itself as well as the subsequent after-effects or symptoms the event gave rise to were of paramount importance to the individual and to the obtaining of a cure.

— [2] Four appendixes are provided for therapists who read this book and are interested in some of the theory that underlies this approach. It may be of interest at this point to read appendix A, "The Formation of Character and Character Armor."

— [3] Nothing in this book should be construed in any way to minimize the vast, important, and complex field of ongoing trauma research and practice--which, for the sake of brevity I will refer to simply as "the work of the trauma community". However, I wish to make a contrasting statement based upon the clinical experience of myself and my psychotherapist colleagues regarding some ways we have devised to pay close attention to and engage relationally with traumatic experience of individuals as it emerges in the psychotherapy consulting room. And further, to suggest some ways any two people engaged in a committed intimate relationship may be able to identify and resolve their post-traumatic experiences.

— [4] This re-living relational process may sound neat and clean—but in practice it's difficult, often baffling and ugly, and usually at least mildly traumatizing to both people involved. I must leave it to Carl Shubs in his forthcoming comprehensive book on trauma to discuss in depth the workings of relational therapy with trauma as it stirs up confusing and often distressing transferences, countertransferences, and resistances.

— [5] I will not in this text undertake a review of the many fascinating facts and findings reported in the research and therapy literature from the trauma community as they are well reported in numerous places elsewhere (for a review see Shubs, in press). Nor will I be taking up any of the fascinating controversies in the literature such as whether childhood trauma and adult onset trauma are fundamentally similar or different, or whether developmental trauma is qualitatively different from focal trauma and so forth. *The focus here will rather be on creating a setting in which people can overcome the inhibiting effects of cumulative developmental trauma in a relational psychotherapy context.*

— [6] Psychological theories, of course, allow us various vantage points from which to understand people and their personal dilemmas according to differing constructs. But in any given intersubjective therapeutic engagement the constructs may or may not prove useful. Further, each psychological theory by its very nature implies something regarding what is to be done about the particular relational concern--another hidden value system to say the least.

[7] Throughout this book I will be referring to the psychological processes of "Transference," "Countertransference," "Resistance," and "Counter-resistance." Transference as the central feature of all psychotherapies—by whatever name it is called—simply refers to the tendency to perceive and respond to relational situations in the present with emotional patterns and templates learned in past relationships. In therapy transference is used to refer to how the client's experience of the therapist is derived from past relational experience. Countertransference refers to how the therapist's experience of the client is derived from the therapist's past relational experiences. There are some who view countertransference feelings as being caused by or reactionary to the client, but present usage favors eliminating that assumption and simply retaining the two words to designate who is experiencing what at a given moment in time, the client or therapist. Resistance *does not mean* resisting therapy or resisting the therapist, but rather resisting the transference and/or countertransference experiencing becoming conscious.

[8] Kingsolver, B. (1990).

[9] The usefulness of the concept of a relational "third person" is elaborated in Appendix D.

[10] See Ogden (1992).

[11] Infant researchers (Beebe and Lachman 2002; Beebe et al. 2005, D.N. Stern 2010) have uncovered many such interactional processes operating in spontaneous interpersonal relationships characterized by mutual affect regulation (Schore 2013, Siegal 1999, 2007).

[12] You will have noted that I alternate between speaking of the "therapeutic" or "overcoming" or "resolving" process as something that can be accomplished in interpersonal/relational psychotherapy, but also as a process that can be often be achieved in any committed intimate relationship. In general, I believe this is so. However, people often find it more convenient and/or effective to hire a personal or couples' therapist. Note that my two (free download) books —*Overcoming Relational Fears* and *Overcoming Relational Fears Workbook* are designed to illustrate how any two can mutually work on identifying and resolving the cumulative developmental trauma.

[13] In making these remarks I do not wish to cast aspersions on time-limited, focal, or empirical approaches to trauma relief. But I wish to make the point that trauma relief is not the same as working over long periods of time in a therapeutic relationship designed to elucidate in transference, resistance, and countertransference the full experiencing of the life-long cascade of traumatic experiences that lie in the depths of any trauma.

[14] Before going on to the Seven Deadly Fears readers who are therapists may want

to step back a few steps and return to our discussions of how we come to know things in psychotherapy. Appendix B discusses Epistemology and the creation of Listening Perspectives.

[15] From a developmental Listening Perspectives standpoint (Appendix B), we understood the role reversals when he was doing to me what had been done to him from the standpoint of the symbiotic listening perspective. But the greatest mileage we got out of all of this was that he was compelled to diminish or rupture any possibility of an emotional connection between us—that is, the organizing perspective in which his early internalized traumas thwarted any attempt on my part to connect emotionally with him—a primitive identification with his mother's rejection of all attempts to relate to her.

[16] The listening perspective (see Appendix B) that was most useful with Carley was the organizing experience because it would seem that her earliest foundational traumas occurred before birth in relation to a womb that somehow failed her. From the material that emerged we can surmise that fetal reactions varied from depressive slumps to frantic attempts to get what she needed. With all of this going on one might also surmise that her thought processes could not have possibly matured in a straightforward, ordinary and reliable way. The therapeutic atmosphere that helped her most was described by Winnicott (1965) as "holding." She has also been repeatedly helped by expressing her murderous rage at me, saying everything she could say to hurt me, to "get even with me" for all the people who have demanded conformity from her, to yell at me, to fire me—and then when the smoke has settled, to find me still there—to have "survived the rage" as Winnicott puts it.

[17] The listening perspective (see Appendix B) that was most helpful in continuing to tune into Christopher's relatedness to me was that of symbiosis wherein there was a stylized way of engaging me and others, i.e., the service mode which left him feeling constantly taken advantage of and/or abused. In time, the organizing listening perspective helped us frame ways that he was terrified of genuine emotional interactions with me so that he found some way to rupture or flee from them. Finally he fell into the organizing level despair of fearing that he was helplessly and hopelessly alone.

[18] This portion of Darrin's analysis was conducted with the listening perspective (see Appendix B) of the symbiosis and role reversal primary identifications. Despite his ability to achieve a good place in the world for himself, following the analysis of the sleeping pill addiction and having to be preoccupied saving mother he became released to be more effectively self-assertive in a number of areas of his life so with hindsight I realized that we had all along been working on that fear as well. However, what follows is an earlier segment of his analysis that necessitated the selfother listening perspective.

[19] The selfobject listening perspective (see Appendix B) was most useful during this phase as we continued to see how compelled he was to talk for me, to dress for me, to flirt with me, and by being sexy to lure me in. This was a

150

cascade of traumatic moments lived in therapy as each glorious attempt gradually caved in to having simply a mutually caring relationship—which he did finally learn to appreciate as real. He didn't need to build himself up to be so great and attractive any more. At that point he confessed his use of sleeping pills and we moved more deeply into his earlier reported mother addiction.

[20] Because of the relationship complexities the therapist reported among Gregory, his wife, his friends and colleagues, his new baby, and his therapist the listening perspective (Appendix A) most useful would likely be the fourth one that highlights cooperative and competitive relations among selves experienced as differentiated and independent. Repression rather than dissociation characterizes this Listening Perspective.

[21] The Independent selves listening perspective (Appendix A) is useful here because Aurora is emotionally mature enough to be able to represent her ambivalent feelings and fears in words and symbols and then to receive verbal interpretations that had a deep emotional impact—transformations in "O".

[22] From the perspective of independent selves, the traumas Marcie re-lived with me are not unlike Gregory's and Aurora's above—well developed people who experience others as differentiated and separate but who, because of excessive needs for cooperation and competition have become repressed and self-depriving. The independent self and other perspective helps most in working with Marcie because her conflicts are mature enough to be embedded in the culturally developed system of symbols. Our deep experiences continued for a number of years to come in the form of simple verbal interpretations—"perhaps in some way we are doing this here?" Then would come the deep thud, the "Oh, my God!" kind of transformative transference interpretation—in Bion's terms a transformation in "O".

[23] Full version of this case is reported in Hedges 1996 and a similar synopsis in Hedges 2013e.

[24] The Listening Perspective of the symbiosis (see Appendix B) was most helpful in this work. We witness here the replication of the two participants' symbiotic scenarios until Sarah has a "new perception" of their mutual enactments of dissociated aspects of themselves (Stern 2010). At that point Sarah retrieves her dissociated anger and "stands against" the symbiotic enactments, thus giving both a new degree of "relatedness flexibility" (Hedges 2013c,d) or "relational freedom" (Stern, in press).

[25] Full version of this case is published in Hedges 1996 and a similar synopsis in Hedges 2013e.

[26] Audrey found the organizing listening perspective (see Appendix B) most useful in working with Anne Marie because her traumas were so early in life she had to compulsively fend off any and all later attempts at contact. While

we have some early history of trauma provided by the family, in my experience we could surmise that she had been unsettled long before the family move but it was not noticed or not remembered. This feels to me almost like another instance of something going awry before birth or shortly after.

[27] Summarized from Ogden, 2002, pp. 95 ff.

— [28] The Listening Perspectives (see Appendix B) here seem to be moving from a merged symbiotic relational experience, through a selfobject consolidation of identity and into a full Oedipal and independent relating mode.

— [29] In my paper "The Riddle of the Psychotic Transference" (2015) I have compared the work of three writers who have addressed this traumatic blocking in early relationships in very different ways—Kalsched's Jungian-oriented "self-care system", Eaton's Bion-based "obstructive object", and Hedges' "the organizing transference".

— [30] Adapted from: Hedges, L.E. (2005). Listening Perspectives for Emotional: Relatedness Memories. *Psychoanal. Inq.*, 25:455-483.

— [31] These charts are explained in detail throughout my published work, see especially 1983, 1992, 1994a, 2000b, 2005, 2013f.

— [32]For elaboration of the concept of intersubjectivity see Stolorow and Atwood 1992 and Benjamin 2004, 2010, 2013.

— [33] The complexities of dissociation, self-states and enactments are dealt with exhaustively in Stern 2010 and Bromberg 2012.

— [35] Foucault, M. (1978). *The History of Sexuality: An Introduction, Volume I*. New York. Random House.

— [36] It is important to note in this brief history of the intersubjective field and the analytic third in English speaking countries, that similar developments were taking place in Spanish, Portuguese, and Italian speaking countries initiated by the Barringers and their work on the bi-personal field in Chile, Argentina and Uruguay, Chuster and others in Brazil, and Ferro in Italy but this is not the place to sketch that history.

# Acknowledgements

As always, I am indebted to the colleagues who study with me at the Listening Perspectives Study Center and the Newport Psychoanalytic Institute, both located in Orange County, California.

Those who have read the text and provided special comments, encouragement and guidance are:

Ann Goldman

Antoinette Eimers

Carl Shubs

Cathy Morrill

Cerina Griffin

Cindy Greenslade

Daniel Uribe

Deborah Lenhart

Greggory Moore

Janis Corbin

Jeanne Lichman

Jeff Schwieger

John Carter

Jolyn Davidson

Judith Besteman

Laura Haynes

Laurie Lucas

Linda Barnhurst

Marty Klein

Robert Davison

Robert Whitcomb

Ted Trubenbach

I am deeply indebted to those who have helped with the manuscript development: Daniel Uribe, Greggory Moore, Monica Mello and Ray Calabrese. Thanks to my longtime friend and publisher Jason Aronson who has since 1980 encouraged me along the way. Melonie Bell skillfully moved the book to publication.

# References

*(Includes a Reading List of Sources Consulted in the Preparation of this Book)*

Abraham, N. and Torok, M. (1994). *The Shell and The Kernel*: Chicago: University of Chicago Press.

Ammaniti, M. and Gallece, V. (2014). *The Birth of Intersubjectivity: Psychodynamics, Neurobiology and the Self*. New York: Norton.

Aron, L. (1991). The Patient's Experience of the Analyst's Subjectivity. *Psychoanal. Dial*. 1-29-51.

_____(2001). A Meeting of Minds: Mutuality in Psychoanalysis. New York: Routledge.

Balint, A. (1943). On Identification. *International Journal of Psycho-Analysis* 24:97-107.

Balint, M. (1930-52 papers, 1985). *Primary Love and Psychoanalytic Technique*. London: Maresfield Press

Beebe, B. and Lachmann, F. M. (2002). *Infant Research and Adult Treatment: A Dyadic Systems Approach*. Hillsdale, NJ: Analytic Press.

Beebe, B., Knoblaunch, S., Rustin, J., and Sorte, D. (2005). *Forms of Intersubjectivity in Infant Research and Adult Treatment*. New York: Other Press.

Benjamin, J. (2004).Beyond the Doer and Done To: An Intersubjective View of Thirdness. *Psychoan. Q*. 22:5-46.

_____. (2010) Where's the gap and what's the difference? The relational view of intersubjectivity, multiple selves, and enactments. *Contemp. Psychoanal*., 46:112-1119.

_____. (2013) *Mutuality*. A paper presented at a UCLA Conference.

155

Bick, E. (1968). *The* experience of the skin in early object-relations. *Int. J. Psycho-Anal.*, 49:484-486.

Bion, W. R. (1962). *Learning from Experience*. New York: Basic Books.

_____. (1992). *Cogitations*. London: Karnac.

Bollas, C. (1987). *Shadow of the Object: Psychoanalysis of the Unthought Known*. London: Free Association Books.

Boon, S., Steele, K. and Hart, O. van der (2011). *Coping With Trauma-related Dissociation: Skills Training For Patients And Their Therapists*. New York: W. W. Norton.

Boulanger, G. (2011). *Wounded By Reality: Understanding and Treating Adult Onset Trauma*. Taylor and Francis. Kindle Edition.

Bromberg, P. M., (1998). *Standing In the Spaces*: Hillsdale, NJ: Analytic Press.

_____. (2006). *Awakening the Dreamer: Clinical Journeys*. Mahwah, NJ: Analytic Press.

_____. ( 2011). *The Shadow of the Tsunami and the Growth of the Relational Mind*: New York: Routledge.

Cohn, J. (1981). Structural consequences of psychic trauma: A new look at 'beyond the pleasure principle'. *Int. J. Psycho-Anal.*, 61; 421-432.

_____. (1985). Trauma and repression*: Psychoanal. Inquiry.*, 5: 163-189.

Cori, J. L. (2009). *Healing from Trauma: A Survivor's Guide to Understanding Your Symptoms and Reclaiming Your Life*. Perseus Books Group. Kindle Edition.

Curtois, C. A. and Ford, J. D., Editors. (2009). *Treating Complex Traumatic Stress Disorders (Adults): An Evidence-Based Guide* . Guilford Publications. Kindle Edition.

David, E. (2011). *PTSD: A Spouse's Perspective: How to Survive in A World of PTSD*. WestBow. Kindle Edition.

Davies, J. M. (1996). Linking the "pre-analytical" with postclassical: integration, dissociation, and the multiplicity of unconscious process. *Contemp. Psychoanal.*, 32:553-576.

_____. (1999). Getting cold feet, defining "safe enough" borders: dissociation, multiplicity, and Integration in the analyst's experience. *Psychoanal Quarterly.* 68:184-208.

_____. (2006). The Times We Sizzle and the Times We Sigh: The Multiple Erotics of Arousal, Anticipation, and Release. *Psychoanal. Dial., 16(6):665-686.*

Davies, J.M., and Frawley, M.G. (1992). Dissociative process and transference-countertransference paradigms in the psychoanalytically oriented treatment of adult survivors of childhood sexual abuse. *Psychoanal. Dial*, 2:5-36.

_____. (1994). *Treating the Adult Survivor of Childhood Sexual Abuse: A Psychoanalytic Perspective.* New York, NY: Basic Books

Davoine, F., and Gaudillière, J. (2004). *History Beyond Trauma: Whereof One Cannot Speak, Thereof One Cannot Stay Silent.* NY: New York Other Press.

Dickes, R. (1965). The defensive function of an altered state of consciousness a hyoid state. *J. Amer. Psychoanal. Assn.*, 13:356-403.

Ferenczi, S. (1920-1933, 1955). Final Contributions to the Problems and Methods of Psychoanalysis. London: Maresfield

Foucault, M. (1985). *The History of Sexuality, Volume I*, Kindle edition.

Freud, A. (1937). *The Ego and the Mechanisms of Defense.* New York:

International Universities Press.

Freud, S. (1915). Observations on transference-love. *Standard Edition* 12:156-173.

_____. (1933). New introductory lectures on psycho-analysis. *Standard Edition* 22:1-184.

Goldner, V. (2006). Let's Do It Again: Further Reflections on Eros and Attachment. *Psychoanal. Dial.*, 16(6):619-637.

Greenberg, J. and Mitchell, S. (1983). *Object Relations in Psychoanalytic Theory.* Boston: Harvard University Press.

Greene, B. (2003). *The Elegant Universe: Superstrings, Hidden Dimensions, and The Quest for the Ultimate Theory.* New York: W. W. Norton.

_____. (2004). *The Fabric of the Cosmos: Space, Time and the Texture of Reality.* New York: Alfred Knopf.

Hedges, L. E. (1983). *Listening Perspectives in Psychotherapy.* Northvale, NJ: Jason Aronson Publishers [Revised Twentieth Anniversary Edition, 2003].

_____. (1992). *Interpreting the Countertransference.* Northvale, NJ: Jason Aronson Publishers.

_____. (1994a). *In Search of the Lost Mother of Infancy.* Northvale, NJ: Jason Aronson Publishers.

_____. (1994b). *Remembering, Repeating, and Working Through Childhood Trauma: The Psychodynamics of Recovered Memories, Multiple Personality, Ritual Abuse, Incest, Molest, and Abduction.* Northvale, NJ: Jason Aronson Publishers.

_____. (1994c). *Working the Organizing experience: Transforming Psychotic, Schizoid, and Autistic States.* Northvale, NJ: Jason Aronson

Publishers.

_____. (1996). *Strategic Emotional Involvement: Using Countertransference Experience in Psychotherapy*. Northvale, NJ: Jason Aronson Publishers.

_____. (2000a,). *Facing the Challenge of Liability in Psychotherapy: Practicing Defensively*. Northvale, NJ: Jason Aronson. [Revised edition 2007]

_____. (2000b). *Terrifying Transferences: Aftershocks of Childhood Trauma*. Northvale, NJ: Jason Aronson Publishers.

_____. (2005). Listening Perspectives for Emotional Relatedness Memories. *Psychoanalytic Inquiry, 25:4, 455-483*.

_____. (2011). *Sex in Psychotherapy; Sexuality, Passion, Love, and Desire in the Therapeutic Encounter*. New York: Routledge.

_____. (2013a). *Cross-Cultural Encounters: Bridging Worlds of Difference* International Psychotherapy Institute e-book. Free download at freepsychotherapybooks.org.

_____. (2013b). *Making Love Last*. International Psychotherapy Institute e-book. Free download at freepsychotherapybooks.org.

_____. (2013c). *Overcoming Relationship Fears*. International Psychotherapy Institute e-book. Free download at freepsychotherapybooks.org.

_____. (2013d). *Overcoming Relationship Fears Workbook*. International Psychotherapy Institute e-book. Free download at freepsychotherapybooks.org.

_____. (2013e). *The Relationship in Psychotherapy and Supervision*. International Psychotherapy Institute e-book. Free download at freepsychotherapybooks.org.

_____. (2013f). *Relational Interventions: Treating Borderline, Bipolar, Schizophrenic, Psychotic, and Characterological Personality Organization*. International Psychotherapy Institute e-book. Free download at freepsychotherapybooks.org.

_____. (2015). The Riddle of the Psychotic Transference. An unpublished address to the International Society for the Study of Schizophrenia and Psychosis in New York City, March 21, 2015.

_____. (1997). Hedges, L., Hilton, R., Hilton, V., Caudill, B. *Therapists At Risk: Perils of the Intimacy of the Therapeutic Relationship*. Northvale, NJ: Jason Aronson Publishers

Heller, L. and Lapierre, A. (2012). *Healing Developmental Trauma: How Early Trauma Affects Self-Regulation, Self-Image, and the Capacity for Relationship*. North Atlantic Books. Kindle Edition.

Hendrix H. (1988). *Getting the Love You Want: A Guide for Couples*. New York: Perennial.

Herman, J. (1992). *Trauma and Recovery: The Aftermath of Violence—from Domestic Abuse to Political Terror*. Kindle Edition.

Hilton, R. (1977). The therapeutic process as it particularly relates to bioenergetics. Workshop handout: Second Year Training Group, Bioenergetics Society of Southern California. January 29, 1977.

_____. (2007). *Relational Somatic Psychotherapy: Collected Essays of Robert Hilton, Ph.D.* Sieck, M. (ed.), San Bernadino, CA; SBGI Press.

Hoge, C. W. (2010). *Once a Warrior—Always a Warrior: Navigating the Transition from Combat to Home—Including Combat Stress, PTSD, and mTBI*. Kindle Edition.

Howell, E. F. (2005). *The Dissociative Mind*. Hillsdale, NJ: Analytic Press.

_____. ( 2011). *Understanding And Treating Dissociative Identity Disorder: A Relational Approach*. New York: Routledge.

James, W. (1901-02). V*arieties of Religious Experience: A Study of Human Nature*. Kindle edition.

Johnson, S. M. (1991). *The Symbiotic Character*. New York: Norton.

Kalsched, D. (1996). T*he Inner World Of Trauma: The Archetypal Defenses Of The Personal Spirit*: New York: Routledge.

_____. (2013). *Trauma and the Soul: A psycho-spiritual approach to human development and its interruption*. New York: Routledge.

Karjala, L. M. (2007). *Understanding Trauma and Dissociation*. Thomas Max Publishing. Kindle Edition.

Karr-Morse, R. and Wiley, M. S. (1997). *Ghosts from The Nursery*. New York: The Atlantic Monthly Press.

Kegan, R. (1994). *In Over Our Heads*: *The Mental Demands of Modern Life*. Cambridge, MA: Harvard University Press.

Kennedy, C. H. (2012). *Military Psychology, Second Edition*. Guilford Press. Kindle Edition.

Khan, M. M. R. (1963). The concept of cumulative trauma. *Psychoanalytic Study of the Child* 18:286-306. New York: International Universities Press.

Kingsolver, B. (1990). *Animal Dreams*. New York: Harper Perennial, pp. 189-191.

Krystal, H. and Krystal, J. H. (1988). *Integration And Self Healing: Affect, Trauma, Alexithymia* Hillsdale, N.J. : Analytic Press.

Levi, P. (2012). *Survival in Auschwitz.* Kindle Edition.

Levine, P. A. (1997). *Waking the Tiger: Healing Trauma.* New York: North Atlantic Books.

_____. (2008). *Healing Trauma.* Kindle Edition.

_____. (2010). *In An Unspoken Voice: How the Body Releases Trauma and Restores Goodness,* Berkeley, CA: North Atlantic Books.

Maroda, K. (1994). *The Power of Countertransference.* Northvale NJ: Aronson.

_____. (1999). *Seduction, Surrender, and Transformation.* Hillsdale, NJ: Analytic Press.

Maté, G. (2010). *In The Realm of Hungry Ghosts: Close Encounters With Addiction.* Berkeley, CA: North Atlantic Books.

Mayer, E.L. (2007). *Extraordinary Knowing: Science, Skepticism, and the Inexplicable Powers of the Human Mind.* New York: Bantam Books.

McClure, K. (2011). *TRAUMA.* Kindle Edition.

Miller, A. (1996,1981). *Prisoners Of Childhood: The Drama Of The Gifted Child And The Search For The True Self.* NY: Basic Books.

Mitchell, S .A. (1988). *Relational Concepts in Psychoanalysis: An Integration.* Boston: Harvard University Press.

_____. (2002). *Can Love Last The Fate of Romance Over Time.* New York: W.W. Norton and Company.

Mitchell. S and Black, M. (2008). *Freud and Beyond: A History of Modern Psychoanalytic Thought.* Kindle edition.

Mitchell, S. and Aron, L. (eds.). (1999). *Relational Psychoanalysis: The Emergence of a Tradition.* New York: Routledge.

Moore, M. S., and Coast, S. W. (1997). The complexity of early trauma: the representation and transformation. *Psychoanal. Inq.*, 17:286-311.

National Institute of Mental Health (2011). *Post-Traumatic Stress Disorder (PTSD)*. Kindle Edition.

Ogden, P., Pain, C., and Minton, K. (2006). *Trauma and the Body: A Sensorimotor Approach to Psychotherapy*. Norton. Kindle Edition.

Ogden, T. (1992). *The Primitive Edge of Experience*. New Jersey: Aronson.

_____. (2002). *Conversations at the Frontier of Dreaming*. New Jersey: Aronson.

Pearce, J. C. (1970, revised 2002). *The Crack in the Cosmic Egg: New Constructs in Mind and Reality*. New York: Park Street Press.

Porges, S. (2011). *The Polyvagal Theory: Neurophysiological Foundations of Emotions, Attachment, Communication and Self-regulation*. New York: Norton.

Reich, W. (1942). *The Discovery of the Orgone, Volume I: The Function of the Orgasm*. New York: Orgone Institute Press. Published as *The Function of the Orgasm; Sex-Economic Problems of Biological Energy*.

_____. (1945). *Character Analysis*. New York: Farrar, Straus and Giroux.

Rorty (1989). *Contingency, Irony, and Solidarity*. London: Cambridge University Press.

Ross, C. A. and Halpern, N. (2011). *Trauma Model Therapy: A Treatment Approach for Trauma, Dissociation, and Complex Comorbidity*. Manitou Communications Inc., Kindle Edition.

Rothschild, B. (2010). *8 Keys to Safe Trauma Recovery*. Norton. Kindle Edition.

Ryle, (1949). *The Concept of Mind*. New York: Barnes and Noble.

Sacks, O. (2012). *Hallucinations*. Knopf Doubleday Publishing Group. Kindle Edition.

Sarnat, J. (1997). Working in the space between psychoanalytic and trauma oriented approaches to stories of abuse. *Gender and Psychoanalysis,.* 2:79-102.

Scaer, R. C. (2001). *The Body Bears The Burden: Trauma, Dissociation, And Disease*. New York: Haworth Medical Press.

Scarry, E. (1985).*The Body in Pain: The Making And Unmaking Of The World*. New York: Oxford University Press

Schore, A.N. (1994). *Affect Regulation and the Origin of the Self: The Neurobiology of Emotional Development*. New Jersey: Lawrence Erlbaum Associates.

_____. (2013). *The Science and The Art Of Psychotherapy*. New York: W.W. Norton.

Searle (2005). *Mind: A Brief Introduction*. London: Oxford University Press.

_____. (1991). *Constructing the Sexual Crucible: An Integration of Sexual and Marital Therapy*. New York: W.W. Norton and Company.

Seaton-Bacon, A. (2000). *I am going to die*. In Hedges 2000b

Shapiro, F. (2012). *Getting Past Your Past: Take Control of Your Life with Self-Help Techniques from EMDR Therapy*. Rodale. Kindle Edition.

Shapiro, R. (2010). *The Trauma Treatment Handbook: Protocols Across the Spectrum* (Norton Professional Books). Norton. Kindle Edition.

Shay, J. (2010a). *Achilles in Vietnam: Combat Trauma and the Undoing of Character*. Scribner. Kindle Edition.

_____. (2010b). *Odysseus in America: Combat Trauma and the Trials of Homecoming*. Scribner. Kindle Edition.

Shengold, L. *Haunted by Parents*. Kindle Edition.

Shubs, C.H. (2008a). Countertransference issues in the assessment and treatment of trauma recovery with victims of violent crime. *Psychoanal. Psychol.*, 25: 156-180.

_____. (2008b) Transference issues concerning victims of violent crime and other traumatic incidents of adulthood. *Psychoanal. Psychol.*, 25:122-141.

_____. (2008c). Treatment issues arising in working with victims of violent crime and other traumatic incidents of adulthood. *Psychoanal. Psychol.*, 25:142-155.

_____. (in press). *Traumatic Experiences of Normal Development: An Intersubjective, Object Relations Listening Perspective on Self, Attachment, Trauma, and Reality*.

Siegal, D. J. (1999). *The Developing Mind: How Relationships and the Brain Interact to Shape Who We Are*. New York: The Guilford Press.

_____. (2007). *The Mindful Brain: Reflection and Attunement in the Cultivation of Well-Being*. New York: W.W. Norton

Soelle, D. *Suffering*. Kindle Edition.

Stark, M. (1994). *Working with Resistance*. New York: Aronson.

_____. (1997). *Modes of Therapeutic Action*. New York: Aronson.

_____. (2015) The Transformative Power of Optimal Stress: From Cursing the Darkness to Lighting a Candle. IPI Ebooks. http://www.freepsychotherapybooks.org.

Stern, D. B. (2003). *Unformulated Experience: From Dissociation to*

*Imagination in Psychoanalysis.* NY: Routledge.

_____. (2010). *Partners In Thought: Working With Unformulated Experience, Dissociation, And Enactment.* NY: Routledge.

_____. (2013). Relational Freedom and Therapeutic Action. *J. Am Psychoan Association* 61:227-254.

Stern, D. N. (2010). *The Present Moment in Psychotherapy and Everyday Life.* New York: Norton

Stolorow, R. D. (2007). *Trauma And Human Existence: Autobiographical, Psychoanalytic, And Philosophical Reflections.* New York: Analytic Press.

Stolorow, R., and Atwood, G. (1992). *Contexts of Being: The Intersubjective Foundations of Psychological Life.* Hillsdale, NJ: Analytic Press.

Stolorow, R., Atwood, G., and Brandchaft, B. (1994). *The Intersubjective Perspective.* Northvale, N]: Jason Aronson.

Sullivan, H. S. (1953). *Interpersonal Theory of Psychiatry.* New York: Norton.

Turner-Miller, S. '*Night, Mother,* In Hedges 1996.

Van der Kolk, B. A., McFarlane, A. C. and Weisæth, Lars. (1996). *Traumatic Stress*: *The Effects Of Overwhelming Experience On Mind, Body, And Society.* New York: Guilford Press.

Wade, N. (2006). *Before The Dawn: Recovering the Lost History of Our Ancestors.* New York: Penguin Books.

_____. (2009). *The Faith Instinct: How Religion Evolved and Why it Endures.* New York: Penguin Books.

_____. (2014). *A Troublesome Inheritance: Genes, Race, and Human History.* New York: Penguin.

Wilson, J. P. (1994). *Countertransference in the Treatment of PTSD*. New York: Guilford Press.

Winnicott, D. (1965). *The Maturational Processes and the Facilitating Environment*. New York: International Universities Press.

Wilson, J. P., Friedman, M. J. and Lindy, J. D. (2001). *Treating Psychological Trauma and PTSD*. New York: Guilford Press.

Wittgenstein, Ludwig (1953). *Philosophical Investigations*. (G. E.M. Anscombe, (tr.) New York: Macmillan Publishing Co., Inc.

Young-Bruehl, E. and Dunbar, C. (2009). *One Hundred Years of Psychoanalysis: A Timeline: 1900-2000*. Toronto, Canada: Caversham Productions.

# About the Author

Lawrence Hedges, Ph.D., Psy.D., ABPP, began seeing patients in 1966 and completed his training in child psycho-analysis in 1973. Since that time his primary occupation has been training and supervising psychotherapists, individually and in groups, on their most difficult cases at the Listening Perspectives Study Center in Orange, California. Dr. Hedges was the Founding Director of the Newport Psychoanalytic Institute in 1983 where he continues to serve as supervising and training analyst. Throughout his career, Dr. Hedges has provided continuing education courses for psycho-therapists throughout the United States and abroad. He has consulted or served as expert witness on more than 400 complaints against psychotherapists in 20 states and has published 21 books on various topics of interest to psychoanalysts and psychoanalytic psychotherapists, three of which have received the Gradiva Award for the best psychoanalytic book of the year. During the 2009 centennial celebration of the International Psychoanalytic Association, his 1992 book, *Interpreting the Countertransference*, was named one of the key contributions in the relational track during the first century of psychoanalysis. In 2015 Dr. Hedges was distinguished by being awarded honorary membership in the American Psychoanalytic Association for his many contributions to psychoanalysis.

Photograph courtesy Marcie Bell

# Other Books Authored and Edited by Lawrence Hedges

***Listening Perspectives in Psychotherapy*** (1983, Revised Edition 2003)

In a fresh and innovative format Hedges organizes an exhaustive overview of contemporary psychoanalytic and object relations theory and clinical practice. "In studying the Listening Perspectives of therapists, the author has identified himself with the idea that one must sometimes change the Listening Perspective and also the interpreting, responding perspective." –Rudolf Ekstein, Ph.D. Contributing therapists: Mary Cook, Susan Courtney, Charles Coverdale, Arlene Dorius, David Garland, Charles Margach, Jenna Riley, and Mary E. Walker. Now available in a Twentieth Anniversary edition, the book has become a classic in the field.

***Interpreting the Countertransference*** (1992)

Hedges boldly studies countertransference as a critical tool for therapeutic understanding. "Hedges clearly and beautifully delineates the components and forms of countertransference and explicates the technique of carefully proffered countertransference informed interventions... [He takes the view] that all countertransferences, no matter how much they belong to the analyst, are unconsciously evoked by the patient." –James Grotstein, M.D. Contributing therapists: Anthony Brailow, Karen K. Redding, and Howard Rogers. Selected as one of the notable contributions to psychoanalysis during its first century—Elisabeth Young-Bruehl and Christine Dunbar (2009).

***In Search of the Lost Mother of Infancy*** *(1994)*

"Organizing transferences" in psychotherapy constitute a living memory of a person's earliest relatedness experiences and failures. Infant research and psychotherapeutic studies from the past two decades now make it possible to define for therapeutic analysis the manifestations of early contact traumas. A history and summary of the Listening Perspective approach to psychotherapy introduces the book. Contributing therapists: Bill Cone, Cecile Dillon, Francie Marais, Sandra Russell, Sabrina Salayz, Jacki Singer, Sean Stewart, Ruth Wimsatt, and Marina Young.

### Working the Organizing Experience: Transforming Psychotic, Schizoid, and Autistic States (1994)

Hedges defines in a clear and impelling manner the most fundamental and treacherous transference phenomena, the emotional experiences retained from the first few months of life. Hedges describes the infant's attempts to reach out and form organizing connections to the interpersonal environment and how those attempts may have been ignored, thwarted, and/or rejected. He demonstrates how people live out these primitive transferences in everyday significant relationships and in the psychotherapy relationship. A critical history of psychotherapy with primitive transferences is contributed by James Grotstein and a case study is contributed by Frances Tustin.

### Remembering, Repeating, and Working Through Childhood Trauma: The Psychodynamics of Recovered Memories, Multiple Personality, Ritual Abuse, Incest, Molest, and Abduction (1994)

Infantile focal as well as strain trauma leave deep psychological scars that show up as symptoms and memories later in life. In psychotherapy people seek to process early experiences that lack ordinary pictoral and narrational representations through a variety of forms of transference and dissociative remembering such as multiple personality, dual relating, archetypal adventures, and false accusations against therapists or other emotionally significant people. "Lawrence Hedges makes a powerful and compelling argument for why traumatic memories recovered during psychotherapy need to be taken seriously. He shows us how and why these memories must be dealt with in thoughtful and responsible ways and not simply uncritically believed and used as tools for destruction." –Elizabeth F. Loftus, Ph.D. Nominated for Gradiva Best Book of the Year Award.

### Strategic Emotional Involvement: Using the Countertransference in Psychotherapy (1996)

Following an overview of contemporary approaches to studying countertransference responsiveness, therapists tell moving stories of how their work came to involve them deeply, emotionally, and not always safely with clients. These comprehensive, intense, and honest reports are the first of their kind ever to be collected and published. Contributing therapists: Anthony Brailow, Suzanne Buchanan, Charles Coverdale, Carolyn Crawford, Jolyn Davidson, Jacqueline Gillespie, Ronald Hirz, Virginia Hunter, Gayle Trenberth, and Sally Turner-Miller.

### Therapists at Risk: Perils of the Intimacy of the Therapeutic Relationship (1997)

Lawrence E. Hedges, Robert Hilton, and Virginia Wink Hilton, long-time trainers of psychotherapists, join hands with attorney O. Brandt Caudill in this *tour de force* which explores the multitude of personal, ethical, and legal risks involved in achieving rewarding transformative connections in psychotherapy today. Relational intimacy is explored through such issues as touching, dualities in relationship, interfacing boundaries, sexuality, countertransference, recovered memories, primitive transferences, false accusations against therapists, and the critical importance of peer support and consultation. The authors clarify the many dynamic issues involved, suggest useful ways of managing the inherent dangers, and work to restore our confidence in and natural enjoyment of the psychotherapeutic process.

### Facing the Challenge of Liability in Psychotherapy: Practicing Defensively (2000, Revised 2017)

In this litigious age, all psychotherapists must protect themselves against the possibility of legal action; malpractice insurance is insufficient and does not begin to address the complexity and the enormity of this critical problem. In this book, Lawrence E. Hedges urges clinicians to practice defensively and provides a course of action that equips them to do so. After working with over a hundred psycho-therapists and attorneys who have fought unwarranted legal and ethical complaints from clients, he has made the fruits of his work available to all therapists. In addition to identifying those patients prone to presenting legal problems, Dr. Hedges provides a series of consent forms (on the accompanying disk), a compelling rationale for using them, and a means of easily introducing them into clinical practice. This book is a wake-up call, a practical, clinically sound response to a frightening reality, and an absolute necessity for all therapists in practice today. Now available in a revised and updated edition. Gradiva Award Best Book of the Year.

### Terrifying Transferences: Aftershocks of Childhood Trauma (2000)

There is a level of stark terror known to one degree or another by all human beings. It silently haunts our lives and occasionally surfaces in therapy. It is this deep-seated fear—often manifest in dreams or fantasies of dismemberment, mutilation, torture, abuse, insanity, rape, or death—that grips us with the terror of being lost forever in time and space or controlled by hostile forces stronger than ourselves. Whether the terror is felt by the client or by the therapist, it has a disorienting, fragmenting, crippling power. How we can look directly into the face of such terror, hold steady, and safely work it through is the subject of *Terrifying Transferences*. Contributing therapists: Linda Barnhurst, John Carter, Shirley Cox, Jolyn Davidson, Virginia Hunter, Michael Reyes, Audrey Seaton-Bacon, Sean Stewart, Gayle Trenberth, and Cynthia Wygal. Gradiva Award Best Book of the Year.

### *Sex in Psychotherapy: Sexuality, Passion, Love, and Desire in the Therapeutic Encounter* (2010)

This book takes a psychodynamic approach to understanding recent technological and theoretical shifts in the field of psychotherapy. Hedges provides an expert overview and analysis of a wide variety of new perspectives on sex, sexuality, gender, and identity; new theories about sex's role in therapy; and new discoveries about the human brain and how it works. Therapists will value Hedges' unique insights into the role of sexuality in therapy, which are grounded in the author's studies of neurology, the history of sexuality, transference, resistance, and countertransference. Clinicians will also appreciate his provocative analyses of influential perspectives on sex, gender, and identity, and his lucid, concrete advice on the practice of therapeutic listening. This is an explosive work of tremendous imagination and scholarship. Hedges speaks the uncomfortable truth that psychotherapy today often reinforces the very paradigms that keep patients stuck in self-defeating, frustrating behavior. He sees sexuality as a vehicle for both therapists and patients to challenge what they think they know about the nature of self and intimacy. This book is a must-read for anyone interested in understanding 21st-century human beings—or in better understanding themselves and their sexuality.

### *Cross-Cultural Encounters: Bridging Worlds of Difference* (2012)

This book is addressed to everyone who regularly encounters people from other cultural, ethnic, socioeconomic, linguistic, and ability groups. Its special focus, however, is aimed at counselors, therapists, and educators since their daily work so often involves highly personal cross-cultural interactive encounters. The running theme throughout the book is the importance of cultivating an attitude of tentative and curious humility and openness in the face of other cultural orientations. I owe a great debt to the many students, clients, and friends with diverse backgrounds who over the years have taught me how embedded I am in my own cultural biases. And who have helped me find ways of momentarily transcending those biases in order to bridge to an inspiring and illuminating intimate personal connection.

### *Overcoming Our Relationship Fears* (2012)

We are all aware that chronic tension saps our energy and contributes to such modern maladies as high blood pressure and tension headaches, but few of us realize that this is caused by muscle constrictions that started as relationship fears in early childhood and live on in our minds and bodies. Overcoming Our Relationship Fears is a user-friendly roadmap for healing our relationships by dealing with our childhood fear reflexes. It is replete with relationship stories to illustrate each fear and how we individually express them. Dr. Hedges shows how to use our own built-in "Aliveness Monitor" to gauge our body's reaction to daily interactions and how they trigger our fears. Exercises in the book will help us release these life-threatening constrictions and reclaim our aliveness with ourselves and others.

### *Overcoming Our Relationship Fears: WORKBOOK* (2013)

Developed to accompany Hedges' Overcoming Relationship Fears, this workbook contains a general introduction to the seven relationship fears that are a part of normal human development along with a series of exercises for individuals and couples who wish to learn to how to release their Body-Mind-Relationship fear reflexes. An Aliveness Journal is provided for charting the way these fears manifest in relationships and body maps to chart their location in each person's body.

### *The Relationship in Psychotherapy and Supervision* (2013)

The sea-change in our understanding of neurobiology, infant research, and interpersonal/relational psychology over the past two decades makes clear that we are first and foremost a relational species. This finding has massive implications for the relational processes involved in teaching and supervising psychotherapy. Clinical theory and technique can be taught didactically. But relationship can only be learned through careful attention to the supervisory encounter itself. This advanced text surveys the psychodynamic and relational processes involved in psychotherapy and supervision.

### *Making Love Last: Creating and Maintaining Intimacy in Long-Term Relationships* (2013)

We have long known that physical and emotional intimacy diminish during the course of long-term relationships. This book deals with the questions, "Why romance fades over time?" And "What can we do about it?" Relational psychologists, neuropsychologists, and anthropologists have devoted the last two decades to the study of these questions with never before available research tools. It is now clear that we are genetically predisposed to search out intersubjective intimacy from birth but that cultural systems of child rearing seriously limit our possibilities for rewarding interpersonal relationships. Anthropological and neurological data suggests that over time we have been essentially a serially monogamous species with an extraordinary capacity for carving out new destinies for ourselves. How can we come to grips with our genetic and neurological heritage while simultaneously transcending our relational history in order to create and sustain exciting romance and nurturing love in long-term relationships? Making Love Last surveys research and theory suggesting that indeed we have the capacity and the means of achieving the lasting love we long for in our committed relationships.

### *Relational Interventions*: *Treating Borderline, Bipolar, Schizophrenic, Psychotic, and Characterological Personality Organization* (2013)

Many clinicians dread working with individuals diagnosed as borderline, bipolar, schizophrenic, psychotic, and character disordered. Often labeled as "high risk" or "difficult", these relational problems and their interpersonal manifestations often require long and intense transformative therapy. In this book Dr. Hedges explains how to address the nature of personality organization in order to flow with—and eventually to enjoy—working at early developmental levels. Dr. Hedges speaks to the client's engagement/disengagement needs, using a relational process-oriented approach, so the therapist can gauge how much and what kind of therapy can be achieved at any point and time.

### *Facing Our Cumulative Developmental Traumas* (2015)

It has now become clear that Cumulative Developmental Trauma is universal. That is, there is no way to grow up and walk the planet without being repeatedly swallowed up by emotional and relational demands from other people. When we become confused, frightened, and overwhelmed our conscious and unconscious minds seek remedies to deal with the situation. Unfortunately, many of the solutions developed in response to intrusive events turn into habitual fear reflexes that get in our way later in life, giving rise to post traumatic stress and relational inhibitions.... This book is about freeing ourselves from the cumulative effects of our life's many relational traumas and the after-effects of those traumas that continue to constrict our capacities for creative, spontaneous, and passionate living.

## Relational Listening: A Handbook

Freud's singular stroke of genius can be simply stated: *When we engage with someone in an emotionally intimate relationship, the deep unconscious emotional/relational habits of both participants become interpersonally engaged and enacted thereby making them potentially available for notice, discussion, transformation, and expansion.*

This *Handbook* is the 20th book in a series edited and/or authored by Dr. Lawrence Hedges and surveys a massive clinical research project extending over 45 years and participated in by more than 400 psychotherapists in case conferences, reading groups and seminars at the Listening Perspectives Study Center and the Newport Psychoanalytic Institute in the Southern California area. The first book in the series, *Listening Perspectives in Psychotherapy* (1983), was widely praised for its comprehensive survey of 100 years of psychoanalytic studies and a 20th anniversary edition was published in 2003. But the important aspect of the book—that the studies were organized according to four different forms of relational listening according to different levels of developmental complexity—went largely unnoticed. Also generally unattended was the critical epistemological shift to perspectivalism which since that time has become better understood. The subsequent books participated in by numerous therapists expand and elaborate these *Relational Listening* perspectives for working clinicians. This *Handbook* provides not only a survey of the findings of the 45-year clinical research project but, more importantly, an overview of the seven developmental levels of relational listening that have consistently been found to provide enhanced psychotherapeutic engagement.

## The Call of Darkness: A Relational Listening Approach to Suicide Intervention (2018)

The White House has declared suicide to be a national and international epidemic and has mandated suicide prevention training for educational and health workers nationwide. *The Call of Darkness* was written in response to that mandate and begins with the awareness that our ability to predict suicide is little better than chance and that at present there are no consistently reliable empirically validated treatment techniques to prevent suicide. However, in the past three decades much has been learned about the dynamics of suicide and promising treatment approaches have been advanced that are slowly yielding clinical as well as empirical results.

In this book, Dr. Hedges presents the groundbreaking work on suicidality of Freud, Jung, Menninger and Shneidman as well as the more recent work of Linehan, Kernberg, Joiner and the attachment theorists along with the features in common that these treatment approaches seem to share. He puts forth a Relational Listening approach regarding the origins of suicidality in a relational/developmental context and will consider their implications for treating, and managing suicidality. The tendencies towards blame and self-blame on the part of survivors raise issues of professional responsibility. Dr Hedges discusses accurate assessment, thorough documentation, appropriate standards of care, and liability management.

# About IPI eBooks

IPI eBooks is a project of the International Psychotherapy Institute. IPI is a non-profit organization dedicated to quality training in psychodynamic psychotherapy and psychoanalysis. Through the resources of IPI, along with voluntary contributions from individuals like you, we are able to provide eBooks relevant to the field of psychotherapy at no cost to our visitors.

Our desire is to provide access to quality texts on the practice of psychotherapy in as wide a manner as possible. You are free to share our books with others as long as no alterations are made to the contents of the books. They must remain in the form in which they were downloaded.

We are always looking for authors in psychotherapy, psychoanalysis, and psychiatry that have work we would like to publish. We offer no royalties but do offer a broad distribution channel to new readers in students and practitioners of psychotherapy. If you have a potential manuscript please contact us at ebooks@theipi.org.

Other books by this publisher:

Rosemary Balsam M.D.

*Sons of Passionate Mothering*

By Richard D. Chessick M.D., Ph.D.

*Freud Teaches Psychotherapy (Second Edition)*

By Lawrence Hedges

*Making Love Last: Creating and Maintaining Intimacy in Long-Term Relationships*

*Overcoming Our Relationship Fears*

*Overcoming Our Relationship Fears Workbook*

*Cross-Cultural Encounters: Bridging Worlds of Difference*

*The Relationship in Psychotherapy and Supervision*

*Relational Interventions*

By Jerome Levin Ph.D.

*Alcoholism in a Shot Glass: What You Need to Know to Understand and Treat Alcohol Abuse*

*The Self and Therapy*

*Grandmoo Goes to Rehab*

*Finding the Cow Within: Using Fantasy to Enrich Your Life*

*Childlessness: How Not Having Children Plays Out Over a Lifetime*

*Treating Parents of Troubled Adult Children*

*Living with Chronic Depression: A Rehabilitation Approach*

By Fred Pine Ph.D.

*Beyond Pluralism: Psychoanalysis and the Workings of Mind*

By Kent Ravenscroft M.D.

*Disaster Psychiatry in Haiti: Training Haitian Medical Professionals*

By Joseph Reppen Ph.D. (Editor)

*Beyond Freud: A Study of Modern Psychoanalytic Theorists*

By David B. Sachar M.D.

*Achieving Success with ADHD: Secrets from an Afflicted Professor of Medicine*

By Fred Sander M.D.

*Individual and Family Therapy*

By Charles A. Sarnoff M.D.

*Theories of Symbolism*

*Symbols in Psychotherapy*

*Symbols in Culture, Art, and Myth*

By Jill Savege Scharff M.D. (Editor)

*Clinical Supervision of Psychoanalytic Psychotherapy*

By Jill Savege Scharff M.D. and David E. Scharff M.D.

*Doctor in the House Seat: Psychoanalysis at the Theatre*

By Gerald Schoenewolf Ph.D.

*Psychoanalytic Centrism*

By Samuel Slipp M.D.

*Anti-Semitism: Its Effect on Freud and Psychoanalysis*

By Imre Szecsödy M.D., Ph.D.

*Supervision and the Making of the Psychoanalyst*

By Vamik Volkan M.D.

*Six Steps in the Treatment of Borderline Personality Organization*

*A Psychoanalytic Process from Beginning to its Termination*

By Judith Warren Ph.D.

*Reading and Therapy: Brush Up Your Shakespeare (and Proust and Hardy)*

Made in the USA
Las Vegas, NV
17 March 2021